I wanted to be a writer, but on a cold Colorado night I shivered with the reality that my "career" was filling tanker trucks with oil. On the rear of one tanker there was a small oval emblem bearing the name Beall, the company that had manufactured it. As I read the word, I separated it into two—be all. It reminded me of Wallace Stevens's poem "The Emperor of Ice Cream," and I recited the poem in my mind. If in the middle of the night, half-frozen, at a dead end job at an oil refinery I could look at the back of a tanker and see words and poetry, it seemed that one day I could be a writer. "Let be be finale of seem."

For Bucky

Contents

Intellectual Property

Everything the Digital-Age Librarian Needs to Know

TIMOTHY LEE WHERRY

AMERICAN LIBRARY ASSOCIATION

Chicago   2008

Composition by ALA Editions in Palatino and Americana using InDesign CS2.

Printed on 50-pound white offset, a pH-neutral stock, and bound in 10-point coated cover stock by McNaughton-Gunn.

The paper used in this publication meets the minimum requirements of American National Standard for Information Sciences—Permanence of Paper for Printed Library Materials, ANSI Z39.48-1992. ∞

Library of Congress Cataloging-in-Publication Data

Wherry, Timothy Lee.
    Intellectual property : everything the digital-age librarian needs
to know / Timothy Lee Wherry.
        p.   cm.
    Includes index.
    ISBN-13: 978-0-8389-0948-5 (alk. paper)
    ISBN-10: 0-8389-0948-5
    1. Intellectual property—United States. I. Title.

    KF2980.W44 2008
    346.7304'8—dc22   2007013893

ISBN-13: 978-0-8389-0948-5
ISBN-10: 0-8389-0948-5

Printed in the United States of America

12   11   10   09   08   5   4   3   2   1

Preface

In 1983 I was hired as engineering librarian at Arizona State University. For ten years prior to that I had worked at Carnegie Mellon University as an engineering librarian and also in private business and industry, so I had a background in chemistry and engineering. At Arizona State I was informed that one of the duties of the engineering librarian was to head the Patent and Trademark Depository Library there—a complete collection of U.S. patents that was made available to the university community and to the public. I knew next to nothing about patents and had to learn fast.

Most of the users of the patent collection were citizens of Arizona who walked into the library with bright eyes and high expectations of riches from patenting an idea they had. My toughest challenge was instructing these people in how to search existing patents, which at the time was a labor-intensive manual process. Most did not have an education beyond high school, and they sought me out because I was the only knowledgeable patent expert they could talk to for free between Dallas and Los Angeles.

To assist people who wanted to do their own patent search, I made handouts on topics such as using the patent index and identifying the field of search. Several years later I had an equivalent position as business and engineering librarian at the Phoenix Public Library and added to my growing collection of patent guides. By the time I arrived at Penn State University in 1990 to become director of the Robert E. Eiche Library, I had more than 200 pages of instructional material. This material formed the basis of my first book, *Patent Searching for Librarians and Inventors*, which was published in 1995 by ALA Editions. Reviews of the book were favorable, and although this first book is now out of print, one large legal firm has labeled it a standard text in introductory patent information. This encouraged me to go further with the topic of intellectual property and to cover copyright and trademarks in my subsequent books, using the same instructional concepts I had first used at Arizona State.

This is my fourth book on intellectual property. The field has changed greatly since 1983, in that the laborious manual searching process for both patents and trademarks has been automated and made available to anyone via the Internet. This in turn has changed the way in which intellectual property is taught and has brought its own challenges. Where once a librarian could say to an amateur patent user, "Go to this call number and get the Index to the U.S. Patent Classification," the instruction for locating the same item on the Web is a process of almost ten steps. That is the trade-off. The process is much easier on the Web, but instructing a person how to use the Internet sites related to intellectual property is tedious to explain. I hope this book will help with that.

I am sincerely thankful to my staff assistant, Mary Hooper, who as always has worked with me to complete this project. Without her assistance in my publication projects I could never finish them. My thanks also to Yehuda Berlinger for his work in writing the intellectual property codes in verse, which appear in appendix A. These poems, which may seem on the surface to be merely whimsical exercises, actually have much practical value. I am also grateful to the University Libraries at Penn State University for their support of my publication activity.

One

Patents, Copyright, and Trademarks

The U.S. Constitution was the first constitution in the world to grant intellectual property rights. It is significant that the wording of the Constitution establishes intellectual property rights for "authors and inventors," but not for their benefit. The purpose is "to promote the progress of science and the useful arts." The benefits of intellectual property are for the sake of society and not the inventor. Article 1, Section 8 of the U.S. Constitution guarantees that "Congress shall have the power . . . to promote the progress of science and useful arts by securing for a limited time to authors and inventors the exclusive rights to their respective writings and discoveries." But although the benefit may be to society, the monetary gain is to the author or inventor. The primary reason that individuals seek intellectual property protection is to gain wealth. When librarians assist library users with queries involving intellectual property, most often the patron is seeking the information not for use in a class paper or to satisfy simple curiosity but to profit from the information.

Each of the creative properties of patents, copyright, and trademarks requires by its nature its own set of laws and methods of control. Together these laws and practices form the subject of intellectual property. The Constitution grants the rights of patent, copyright, and trademark protection, but the manner in which each is secured, the time frame allowed for protection, and other details are regulated by laws that were written later. From the simple statement in Article 1, Section 8 has come several branches of law, thousands of court cases, and entire volumes of the U.S. Code. For example, Title 17 of the U.S. Code is devoted exclusively to copyright.

In very few instances are librarians able to answer questions about intellectual property in clear and definitive language. Those who work with intellectual property are often faced with the "what if" question. If Person A is told that she cannot download another's copyrighted image from the Internet and then post it on her website for distribution worldwide, immediately the next question from Person A is, "Well, what if . . . ?" Often the circumstances of the individual situation will alter the application and meaning of the law.

Differences among Types of Intellectual Property

In their simplest form patents concern functional things, copyrights concern artistic expression, and trademarks protect the word or symbol that identifies a given product in the mind of the consumer. The Patent and Trademark Office (PTO) administers patents and trademarks, and the Copyright Office, a unit of the Library of Congress, administers copyrights.

Patents

Patents are divided into three types: utility patents (which are divided into three categories: mechanical, electrical, and chemical), design patents, and plant patents.

Utility patents are those inventions that are normally thought of as machines, such as a cell phone or an MP3 player. Design patents are granted to the design of a functional thing. This has caused a great deal of misunderstanding, since the term *design* connotes artistic expression, which is covered by copyright. The difference is that a design patent is granted on an item that serves a function. A vase shaped like a tree would be design patented, not copyrighted, since it performs a function—it holds flowers. Copyright is granted on items that are purely artistic, like a sculpture of a tree. The key to understanding the difference between design patents and copyright is that in order for a creative thing to be design patented, it must have a useful purpose, or function. Things that are copyrighted are the physical form of a thing that is purely artistic, like a sculpture, a painting, or a book.

A plant patent is granted on a new type of plant that is created by human intervention and is created asexually. Many people know about "patent roses." These are roses that are created by horticultural manipulation and are not naturally occurring plants. A person who finds a new kind of plant growing wild in a field could not patent that plant, but a person who can show that she has taken cuttings and manipulated generations of several plants to create a new plant could patent the new plant.

Patents are extremely valuable to universities. Academics are regularly faced with the conflict between the academy's desire to freely distribute and share information on new discoveries by publishing a conference paper and the university's concern for keeping secret a discovery that may lead to millions of dollars for the university. The Harvard mouse, which is a patented animal that is prone to cancer, has meant millions of dollars in royalty payments to Harvard University. University patenting has hit a fever pitch in the past decade because of this potential for profit. In 2005 the university to receive the most patents was the University of California, with 424 patents—although legally universities cannot receive patents. Only individuals can own patents.

Copyright

Copyright concerns artistic or literary expression. The thing that is copyrighted can be a book, a picture, a sculpture, a painting, jewelry designs, a motion picture, music, or anything that is the result of a person's creative mind that takes a physical shape and has no function other than the beauty of the thing itself. Unlike a patent, the thing being copyrighted must be functionless or useless. Copyright is protection on the expression of an artistic idea that is "fixed in any tangible medium of expression," according to Title 17, Section 102 of the U.S. Code. "Fixed" means that the artistic expression is written on paper or painted on canvas or shaped in stone. "Fixed" means that the idea in the artist or author's mind must take a physical form. Copyright grants five primary rights to the copyright holder: the right to make copies, the right to prepare derivative works, the right to distribute copies, the right to perform the work publicly, and the right to display the work publicly.

The issue that causes the most confusion in the mind of the public involves slogans or sayings. Those who come up with a catchy phrase like "So many books, so little time" picture the phrase on bumper stickers or on T-shirts that they will sell in order to make them rich. Often librarians will be asked to assist a person who wants to "copyright a saying for a bumper sticker." However, one of the things that cannot be copyrighted is a slogan or saying. A slogan can only be trademarked and must follow the requirements for trademarks, which are outlined in the chapter in this book on trademarks.

Those in education have the biggest problem with copyright since it is believed, mistakenly, that as long as a copyrighted work is used for instruction it is allowed under the concept of "fair use." Fair use is that part of the copyright law that allows a waiver of the copyright protections under certain circumstances. A full explanation of fair use is in the chapter on copyright.

Copyright is the most difficult area of intellectual property for librarians. Patents have a more defined procedure for granting protection, and granted patents can be located by a structured search. Trademarks can also be searched to verify their existence, and the existence of a trademark is easy to verify by locating it on a product or service. Copyright, however, does not have to be registered; its ownership is often not clear; the non-licensed use of copyright known as "fair use" is very vague; and what is allowed or not allowed is based on established court cases and not the imprimatur of the federal government.

Information is both free and expensive. It is free because a posted document on the Internet is so cheap and easy to download, copy, distribute, recombine, and transfer. But information is also expensive because of its value to the recipient. This leads to ongoing debates about the price of information, copyright, the ethics of casual copying and distribution, and new technologies that only make the struggle to define what is legal more difficult.

Trademarks

Trademarks concern identification. The current trademark law, the Lanham Act, was enacted in 1946 and is still in effect. According to Lanham, a trademark is "any word, name, symbol, or device, or any combination thereof, and used by a manufacturer or merchant to identify his goods, and distinguish them manufactured or sold by others."

Trademarks are also broken down into types. A trademark may be a brand name, trade dress, service mark, certification mark, or collective mark. For example, a brand name would be Coca-Cola; a trade dress would be the shape of the Coca-Cola bottle (see figure 1-1); a service mark would be the lettering that describes TIAA-CREF financial services; a certification mark would be the UL symbol that identifies electrical devices that have been tested by Underwriters Laboratories and have met certain standards; and a collective mark could be the CPA lettering after an accountant's name that designates an association or collective such as Certified Public Accountants. For purposes of simplicity, all types of trademarks are referred to as "trademarks" or "marks." An example of a well-known trademark would be the Colonel Sanders image for Kentucky Fried Chicken. One of the rules of

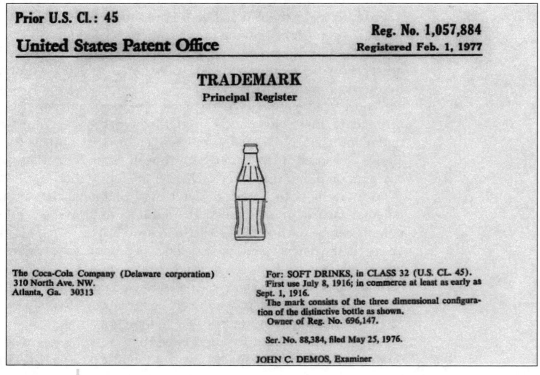

Figure 1-1

Coca-Cola bottle trademark

intellectual property is that phrases such as De Beers's "A Diamond Is Forever" and Capital One's "What's in Your Wallet?" are not permissible for copyright protection but may be trademarks.

Examples of Intellectual Property Types

The easiest way to define how protection applies to each type of intellectual property is with an example of a single object that would be patented, trademarked, and copyrighted. Crest toothpaste is an example of a product that is protected by all three major types of intellectual property. Crest toothpaste has a patented formula. The name Crest is a trademark. The red and blue Crest lettering and the artwork on the Crest tube and box are copyrighted.

In 1910 the sculptor Charles Sykes created a sculpture that he called *The Spirit of Ecstasy.* The sculpture was licensed by Rolls-Royce Automobiles to later become the Rolls-Royce automobile's hood ornament, known as "The Flying Lady," and it was adopted as a corporate symbol. "The Flying Lady" is protected by a copyright since it was, at its inception, a sculpture. "The Flying Lady" image is also the registered trademark of the Rolls-Royce Automobile Company. But how does a patent protect "The Flying Lady," since it seems to be a purely decorative and nonfunctional piece of art? Originally, the sculpture functioned as the automobile's radiator cap. In this capacity, a design patent protected it.

Technology and Intellectual Property

We can best introduce the issues involving the digital age and intellectual property by examining how the courts view cases that involve existing intellectual property law as it bumps into issues created by new technology. None of the three types of intellectual property functions in a perfect environment. Whenever new technology is introduced, intellectual property law is often left behind, since new technology brings new challenges. In addition, significant legal cases move with glacial speed through the court system, leaving intellectual property decisions in limbo for years.

Patents

In 1976 the new technology of the videocassette recorder (VCR) spawned the landmark case of *Sony v. Universal City Studios.* At issue was the Sony Betamax VCR. VCRs allowed the public to freely copy televised motion pictures—*copyrighted* televised motion pictures. Sony was sued by Universal Studios for contributory infringement, which meant that Sony itself was not infringing on copyright but that the Betamax was allowing others to infringe. The case finally came before the U.S. Supreme Court in 1984. In those eight years the Betamax had fallen out of favor with consumers in favor of the competing VCR technology of VHS, but the legal issue was still significant. The Court decided two important concepts: that since consumers were simply time shifting—copying broadcasts to allow them to be seen at a later time—copying programs from television was fair use; and since the technology itself was not performing any illegal action, it was legal. This Court decision created the movie rental industry, and it was also a boon to the movie industry, which now typically generates over 60 percent of the profit on a motion picture from video rentals.

In March 2006 Research in Motion paid NTP, Inc., $612.5 million to settle a patent infringement suit. Research in Motion is the manufacturer of the popular BlackBerry e-mail/mobile phone device; however, because of the claims of NTP and another company against Research in Motion, it was never issued a patent for its device. Had Research in Motion not settled, the suit might have shut down the entire BlackBerry network until the dispute was resolved.

In another case, just weeks after Apple announced a two-for-one stock split in 2006, the company faced intellectual property challenges related to its lucrative iPod device and iTunes music store. Two small companies claimed that Apple's iPod violated patents they owned. One of those companies was Chicago-based Advanced Audio Devices, which sued Apple in federal court for allegedly violating its patents for a "music jukebox." The U.S. Patent and Trademark Office had granted Advanced Audio Devices a patent in July 2003 for a music jukebox designed for storing a music library. The company had originally filed for the patent in 2001. Apple applied for its patent, application number 20,030,995,096, in October 2002, but because of the legal challenges, it was never issued a patent.

Apple shipped 4.58 million iPods during the first quarter of 2005 alone. What's more, Apple announced in 2007 that iTunes music downloads had surpassed 2 billion. That works out to 5 million songs per day, or 58 songs per second. Among top music retailers Apple ranks fourth behind Wal-Mart, Best Buy, and Target. Even a settlement for a modest percentage of Apple's profits on the iPod and music downloads could be hundreds of millions of dollars.

The current Supreme Court could radically alter patent law. In 2006 the high court agreed to rule on more patent cases than it has in four decades. A possible reason for this interest in intellectual property is that the courts currently place injunctions on patent infringers for transgressions. Because of the injunctions, defendants have been forced to settle quickly with patent holders and pay huge sums, as seen in the BlackBerry example. The decision to hear so many patent cases could be a signal that the Court wants to tip the balance of power away from patent holders for the good of society. Some would argue that this was the original purpose of Article 1, Section 8—the good of society rather than the benefit of the individual.

In November 2006 the Court agreed to hear arguments on the definition of the term *obvious* as it relates to granting patents. Patent law says that something that is obvious is not patentable, but the definition is ambiguous. This has led to an explosion of patent suits as companies have made claims on other companies' inventions that may include parts of a previous invention, making the new patent an obvious combination of two patents, as in the case of KSR explained in the chapter on patents.

Copyright

Trouble is also brewing in copyright law because of technology. Much of the contention seems to revolve around Google. High-profile cases include Google's defense of its library print project, its application of thumbnail images, and its caching of copyrighted materials. At issue is the problem of the ownership of images that have been altered or manipulated in some way by technology, which have blurred the line between original copyright ownership and the ownership of digitally manipulated and distributed images.

In one case, *Field v. Google,* Google was sued for caching, or archiving, material found on the Internet. For example, if a poem is posted on a Usenet bulletin board and a user queries Google, the search results may bring up a hyperlink within Google to the bulletin board that has posted the poem. In effect this is providing a copy of the poem to the searcher. The right to reproduce a work is a right granted only to the copyright holder. So is caching a violation of copyright? Yes and no. As was stated earlier, very little is definitive in intellectual property. In some cases caching is infringement; in others it is not. This particular case was based on one of the five rights of copyright: the one that allows only the copyright holder to make copies.

In this case, Google's actions closely paralleled the actions of an Internet service provider (ISP) such as AOL. According to the 1998 Digital Millennium Copyright Act (DMCA), which is explained more fully in the chapter on copyright, an ISP is not responsible for the actions of those who may use its service for illegal purposes. This follows the concept first pointed out in the *Sony v. Universal City Studios* case discussed earlier, that providing the technology to allow copying is not the same as making a copy.

The law may also work the other way around. In another case, *Perfect 10 v. Google,* at issue was the right of the copyright holder to *display* a copyrighted work. In this case Google had thumbnails of copyrighted pictures belonging to Perfect 10. Although Google linked to a thumbnail copy of the picture, it did not actually display a full-sized copy of the picture. A person could print a full-sized copy of the picture but in doing so reverted to the Perfect 10 website. So Google was acting as an ISP in providing the means of copying but did not provide the original picture and thus had safe harbor. At issue in this case was the right of the copyright holder to display a copyrighted work and not the issue of copying the work. Google certainly displayed the thumbnail picture, but adding to the issues in the case is whether Google provided the thumbnail from its cache or if Google merely pointed to the website that contained the copyrighted picture. Google was found liable in district court but has appealed the ruling, and the case will take many years to work its way through the courts.

Although Google is not the only company that is legally wrangling with intellectual property issues, its cases are highly visible because of the familiarity of its services to anybody who uses the Internet. Any company that is on the cutting edge of the digital age will sooner or later run into legal issues concerning intellectual property. The Google examples are valuable as illustrations because the issues at stake are ones that are familiar to librarians and to the public that libraries serve.

Trademarks

In one trademark suit the litigant, American Blinds and Wallpaper Factory (ABW), sued not only Google but also AOL, Netscape, CompuServe, Ask Jeeves, and Earthlink. At issue was the use of "Adwords," which are words or phases that are linked to an advertiser's website. The Adword program generates most of Google's profit. Inputting the Adword as part of a search triggers the advertiser's link to appear at the top right-hand side of the results page. For example, a search for "ALA poster" will bring up in the Adwords area a group of advertisers who have paid Google to be displayed every time a word that they have identified is part of a search. This particular search brings up links to Art.com, AllPosters.com, and eBay.

At issue is the use of the trademark "American Blinds and Wallpaper Factory" and of "Decorate Today," which is the trademarked URL of ABW. A searcher typing in "decorate today" is directed to the ABW website, but because of Adwords, links to competitors' websites are also listed, not as part of the results of the search but as a supplement to the search appearing in the Adwords section of the results page. So ABW's trademark is being used to inform searchers of ABW's competitors. In legal terms this is known as "dilution" and also as plain old trademark infringement—using another's trademark to advertise a competitor's goods and services. Also at issue in this particular case is the lack of intelligence of Google's search engine. Although a search for "American Blinds and Wallpaper" would bring up other manufacturers of blinds, a search for "American blind person" would also bring up ABW competitors. What is lacking is the intent on Google's part to dilute the trademark.

Another concept in trademark law is the ability to register similar trademarks if each is in a different area. For example, there are forty-two classes of goods and services. If a person trademarked the term "White Glove Care" in the category that included car washes, another person could trademark "White Glove Care" in the category that included insurance services. A full list of trademark categories appears in the chapter on trademarks.

One of the things that cannot be trademarked is a descriptive word or phrase. The Ninth Circuit Court verified this in the *Park'N Fly v. Dollar Park and Fly* case, in which Dollar Park and Fly was found not to be infringing on the Park'N Fly trademark. This case helped to develop the concept of "nominative fair use," which allows the use of a registered trademark by others if the mark is simply descriptive. *Park and fly* is descriptive because people do park and fly at an airport, so the trademark cannot be effectively protected. Another example is that if a person manufactured a battery-operated spinning spaghetti fork, she could not market it under the trademarked name "Spinning Spaghetti Fork," since that name would be simply descriptive.

In the 1970s Cities Service Company was fighting trademark battles continually because the company's name was fairly generic and difficult to protect. The company programmed a computer to come up with five- to seven-letter variations of possible words that could be made from the letters in Cities Service and additional letters to make the word pronounceable. The one chosen was Citgo, and the company has used that name ever since. This was not simply a ploy to eliminate trademark infringement cases, but it does indeed help eliminate them. Trademark infringement occurs when a word or phrase is confusingly similar to an existing trademark. If a company uses a completely new word, the chances of its infringing on an existing trademark are virtually nonexistent. This is the technique that Standard Oil used. In various parts of the country the company was known as Esso or Standard Oil, and it wanted to consolidate these names in such a way as to avoid trademark suits and establish a unique name. It came up with Exxon, which has no meaning other than the name of the company.

These few examples illustrate just some of the issues that arise when intellectual property confronts technology. More examples and important concepts for librarians are provided in the following chapters. Historically, when intellectual property has faced technology, intellectual property law has usually won out. But in this new digital environment it is clear that there are new challenges.

Two

Patents

A patent is a contract between society and an inventor. In the interest of spurring innovation, society agrees to protect an inventor's control over an invention, and in return the inventor must publicly disclose the details of the invention. The information made available thus potentially spurs further innovation.

Types of Patents

As stated previously, there are three types of patents: utility patents, design patents, and plant patents. Utility patents are what most people think of as an invention, for example, an iPod or a cell phone. Utility patents are further broken down into three types: chemical, mechanical, and electrical. All utility patents are squeezed into these three categories even when their placement is not obvious. Computer software, for example, in some instances is patentable as a set of instructions to an electrical component, thereby making the patent fall into the electrical category.

Pharmaceuticals are placed in the chemical patent category. The United States is one of the few countries that allow patents on drugs. Other nations feel that drugs are beneficial to society and should not be proprietary products. Of course, in a large capitalist society, having a monopoly on a big-selling drug makes stockholders happy. Gene-splicing techniques or the Harvard mouse, a genetically engineered mouse, also fall into the chemical category.

Design patents are granted on the appearance of something. For example, in making a computer monitor with a thin plastic frame around the screen instead of a large plastic screen border, an inventor does not reinvent the monitor but only changes its appearance. The design can be protected, not the concept of the monitor itself.

Plant patents are granted on bushes, trees, roses, and other plants that are reproduced asexually with human intervention, which is to say that they do not occur naturally and are not propagated by tubers. Patent roses, for example, are a particular type or color of rose that are protected from duplication by other horticulturalists. Interestingly, since a patentable part of a plant is its color, these patents are issued in color booklets rather than in the standard black-and-white patent document. A problem for librarians is that microfilm of plant patents is unavailable, because the drawings must be in color. A further problem is that when searching plant patents on the Patent and Trademark Office website, the images are in black and white.

A Word about Software Patents

Software can be either patented or copyrighted, and there is an ongoing debate as to where software properly belongs within intellectual property categories. When software is copyrighted, this regulates the direct copying of the program code. When software is patented, it covers the programming method itself. The issue arose with the first software patent application ever filed (in 1962), which related to solving simultaneous linear equations. The Patent and Trademark Office traditionally considered software to be not patentable because patents are only granted on processes, machines, articles of manufacture, and compositions of matter. Patents are not granted on scientific truths or mathematical expressions of those truths.

The PTO's position was challenged in a landmark 1981 case, *Diamond v. Diehr*. The invention in question incorporated software that was used to time the curing of rubber, but it had other uses in the actual manipulation of rubber products. So as part of a device to mold rubber, it was patentable. In simple terms, algorithms themselves are not patentable, since they are mathematical expressions of scientific truths, but devices that use the algorithms are patentable. The debate is ongoing as to where software properly belongs.

Requirements for Patents

There are four requirements for a U.S. patent. First, the invention must be the first of its kind, and not only the first of its kind but the first any person has even heard of the idea. There is a legal concept called "anticipation." This means that an invention may not have been sold or disclosed anywhere in print or by word of mouth by the inventor or anyone else for longer than one year before an application is submitted. The rationale for this rule follows the concept behind patenting in the United States as opposed to patenting in some other industrialized nations: in the United States the person who first invents a device has the right to patent, whereas in some other countries, Japan, for example, the first person to obtain the patent has the right to the invention. To protect this right in the United States, it is then necessary to ensure that the idea is an original thought of the inventor by verifying that the idea did not exist before application was made. There must be no other patent like it not only in the United States but in the world. There must also be no mention of the invention in any printed matter, such as a magazine or newspaper, or in any way to show that the invention was in public use.

Second, an invention eligible for patenting must be useful. This means that a patented invention must have a function. This has never been a problem. If an invention is not useful, an inventor is unlikely to go to the time and expense of obtaining a patent for it. Of course, usefulness is sometimes a questionable call. The only exception to the concept of usefulness would be in the case of plant patents, where the plant is simply attractive and performs no function.

Third, the invention must not be obvious to others of ordinary skill in the field in which the patent pertains. This is the ultimate condition and attempts to measure an abstract thing: the technical accomplishment reflected in the invention. For example, substituting one material for another or changes in size are usually not patentable, with the exception being design patents. Combining patents to create a new patent is usually not allowed. Thomas Jefferson said that a man "has a right to use his knife to cut his meat; a fork to hold it; may a patentee take from him the right to combine their use on the same subject?" However, the minor changes by which a new invention accomplishes the same end as an existing patented invention are the decision of the patent examiner, and this demonstrates why examiners must have a technical background.

How to determine when an invention is obvious is one of the most critical and contentious issues in patenting. Critics of the PTO argue that over the past few years the obviousness test has been lowered and this has created many junk patents. One of these junk patents, a toy that a dog may carry in its mouth, is nothing more than a rubber stick (figure 2-1). Another, a method for exercising cats, is simply teasing the cat with a laser pen (figure 2-2). Patent number 6,004,596 is for a peanut butter and jelly sandwich and has been the focus of a suit between J. M. Smucker Company, which markets a crustless peanut butter and jelly sandwich, and Albie's Foods, an Ohio company that owns the patent on a crustless peanut butter and jelly sandwich.

In 2001 KSR International Company, a Canadian firm, manufactured gas pedals for 2003 General Motors vehicles. But not just any pedals. These pedals were adjustable to accommodate drivers of differing heights and used an electronic signal rather than a mechanical cable to change engine speed. Both features had been known in automotive circles for a number of years and were patented. Teleflex, a Pennsylvania company, held patents on adjustable pedals and electronic sensors and maintained that KSR's manufacturing any combination of these would

US006360693B1

(12) **United States Patent**
Long, III

(10) **Patent No.:** US 6,360,693 B1
(45) **Date of Patent:** Mar. 26, 2002

(54) **ANIMAL TOY**

(76) Inventor: **Ross Eugene Long, III,** 4732 Reinhardt Dr., Oakland, CA (US) 94619

(*) Notice: Subject to any disclaimer, the term of this patent is extended or adjusted under 35 U.S.C. 154(b) by 0 days.

(21) Appl. No.: **09/454,229**

(22) Filed: **Dec. 2, 1999**

(51) Int. Cl.[7] A01K 29/00
(52) U.S. Cl. 119/707
(58) Field of Search 119/702, 707, 119/709, 710, 711, 467, 468, 256, 268

(56) **References Cited**

U.S. PATENT DOCUMENTS

1,006,182 A	*	10/1911	Cousin	119/710
1,022,113 A	*	4/1912	Smith	119/710
3,830,202 A	*	8/1974	Garrison	119/710
4,202,922 A	*	5/1980	Osment	428/18
5,018,480 A	*	5/1991	Goldman et al.	119/26
RE34,352 E	*	8/1993	Markham et al.	119/710
5,752,463 A	*	5/1998	Jenkins	119/57.8
5,819,687 A	*	10/1998	Lister	119/52.1

* cited by examiner

Primary Examiner—Thomas Price

(57) **ABSTRACT**

An apparatus for use as a toy by an animal, for example a dog, to either fetch carry or chew includes a main section with at least one protrusion extending therefrom that resembles a branch in appearance. The toy is formed of any of a number of materials including rubber, plastic, or wood including wood composites and is solid. It is either rigid or flexible. A flavoring (scent) is added, if desired. The toy is adapted to float by including a material therein that is lighter than water or it is adapted to glow in the dark, as desired, by the addition of a fluorescent material that is either included in the material from which the toy is made or the flourescent material is applied thereto as a coating. The toy may be segmented (i.e., notched) so as to break off into smaller segments, as is useful for smaller animals or, alternatively, to extend the life of the toy. Various textured surfaces including camouflage colorings are anticipated as are straight or curved main sections. The toy may be formed of any desired material, as described, so as to be edible by the animal.

20 Claims, 3 Drawing Sheets

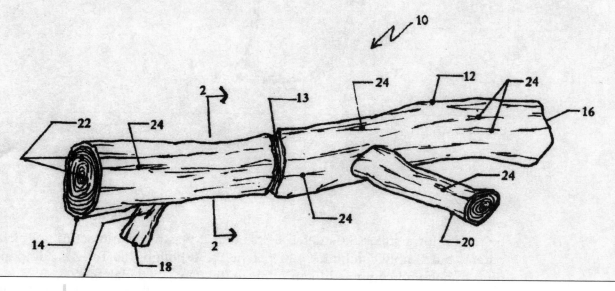

Figure 2-1

Patent for a stick toy for dogs

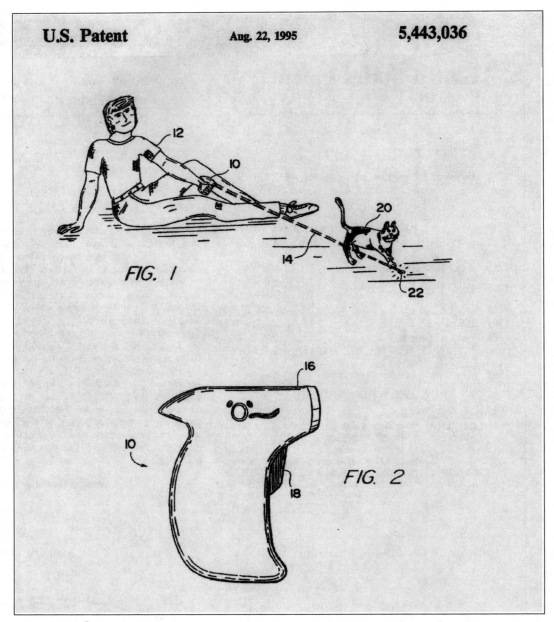

FIG. 1

FIG. 2

Figure 2-2

Patent for laser-pen method of playing with a cat

be reason for a suit. KSR's defense was that it was not manufacturing Teleflex's patents but simply combining two patents. KSR bought the Teleflex components off the shelf and combined them to make the new gas pedal. Since U.S. law does not allow patents for inventions that are obvious, KSR argued that it should be permitted to manufacture a combination gas pedal and sensor, since the company was obviously combining two ideas and was not creating a new patent. KSR's argument is that Teleflex may as well have patented the combination of a refrigerator and a lightbulb. The Supreme Court ruled in favor of KSR in April 2007.

The fourth requirement for a patent is that the invention must be able to be reproduced by somebody of average skill with the technology involved.

Patent Pending

Often seen on new products, the phrase *patent pending* means that a patent application has been submitted; this is simply a marketing technique to give the manufacturer a head start. The time from patent application to patent issue is now an average of thirty-one months. Since the inventor of the product is first in line for a possible patent, others are discouraged from applying for a patent on the same product while the patent application is being examined. The phrase *patent pending* offers no protection under the law because a patent application may be rejected, but it is unlawful to mark an item *patent pending* if an application is not on file. During the application process, patent forms are kept in secret so that others may not copy the invention. Employees of the PTO are prohibited from owning patents to further ensure the confidentiality of the process.

Patent Expiration

A patent is good for twenty years from the date of issue. A patent cannot be renewed or extended except by an act of Congress. After twenty years the patent becomes public property and anyone can copy or manufacture the invention. In order to keep a patent in effect, the inventor pays maintenance fees for those twenty years. Once a patent has been granted, even though it has expired, the same device cannot be patented again by the original inventor or by another.

One question that librarians are often asked about patent expiration is: if the patent on the formula for Crest toothpaste expired after twenty years and everybody can copy the formula, how does Crest manage to retain its customers, since the same toothpaste would be available from other manufacturers at a cheaper price? The answer is that the company comes up with a new, improved Crest, which has an altered chemical formula and fights tartar or whitens one's teeth, and is granted a new patent. Who then would want to buy the old, unimproved Crest?

The same concept holds for drug manufacturers. A successful drug such as Viagra can make a lot of money for a pharmaceutical company, but after twenty years the company is pressured to come up with a new erectile dysfunction drug, since other drug companies may then manufacture Viagra as a generic drug. Generic drugs are available inexpensively from other drug companies because the patent has expired.

Patentee and Assignee

A patentee is the person who is named as the inventor in the patent. Only named persons may hold patents; business entities or corporations may not. An assignee is a person or company to whom the patentee has sold rights to the invention.

The patentee does not have to be a single individual; it may be several people holding joint rights if they all contributed intellectually to the invention. The phrase *contributed intellectually* means that they were involved in the actual inventing of the device. To illustrate this distinction, if a brother gives an inventor $1,000 to finance the development of a widget but has no input in the actual inventing of the widget, the patent cannot be issued in both the inventor and brother's names, nor can the brother be the assignee unless he has filed forms with the PTO showing that he has purchased rights to the invention. Only the true inventor can obtain a patent.

After the Patent and Trademark Office grants a patent, it usually does not act on an inventor's behalf except in cases of reexaminations or reissues. Any violation of an inventor's patent rights is pursued through the courts and not through the PTO. Many inventors have been ruined economically by fighting patent infringement cases in the courts, and some patentees attempt to sell their patents if litigation is pending, since it then becomes the assignee's responsibility to defend the patent in court.

Reissued Patents

When patents are issued, the patent document contains many pieces of information: the inventor's name; a brief description of the invention; several drawings of the invention from differing angles, including close-ups of components or subassemblies; "claims," which are the words that explain precisely what is new and unique about the invention; a long description of the invention and sometimes a brief background of the technology or need that necessitated it; and a short list of related patents and classifications searched. Occasionally a patent is issued that contains a mistake in one of these important components. There may be a mistake in the wording of a claim, for example. When this happens the inventor fixes the problem and a new patent number is assigned. In lists of patent numbers that a searcher may use, these reissued patents are easily identified by the letters RE before the number.

A Growing Problem

According to the U.S. Department of Commerce's *Technology Assessment and Forecast Report,* the Patent and Trademark Office received 382,139 patent applications in 2004. Since 1985 the annual number of patent applications has nearly tripled. In 2004, 181,302 patents were issued, so the odds of an application being granted a patent are about 50 percent. There are approximately 4,800 patent examiners (an increase of 1,000 examiners in the past three years) who decide whether an application will be granted a patent, so each patent examiner handles about 100 patents a year on average. This is twice the workload of patent examiners in European countries. Meanwhile, patent litigation has been increasing since 1982, when Congress created a special court to handle patent cases. Between 1983 and 2004 patent suits nearly tripled.

In 1976 the 4,000,000th patent was issued; in 1991 the 5,000,000th patent was issued; the 6,000,000th was issued in 1999 and the 7,000,000th on February 14, 2006. Clearly the number of patents granted each year is increasing dramatically. In the past 36 years there have been as many patents issued as were issued in the first 134 years of the U.S. patent system. Also of concern is the number of foreign-owned U.S. patents issued annually. In 2004, 48 percent of all issued patents were owned by citizens of other countries. *On average* a patent generates just $50,000 in sales, and 57 percent of inventors sell their creation for a profit; however, only about 2 percent of issued patents ever make a dime for their inventors.

Part of the cause for the lack of profit on a patent is the misguided vision of some inventors and the consequences of vanity. People have many lame reasons for filing patents. Some just want to swell their résumés. Others figure that if they file twenty patents, maybe one will turn a profit. There is an entire cottage industry of "hobby patenting": people who patent ideas continually whether they are economically viable or not. The idea is that in the future if technology favors them, they can become wealthy from a seemingly worthless patent. The lore of patents is filled with brilliant, sly people who became rich from hobby patents. Many will patent an economically unviable thing just for ego satisfaction.

There are also patent "trolls." A patent troll is an individual or company that buys up patents in hopes of suing people who may infringe on their patent. In 2002 colleges and porn site operators and newspapers began receiving cease and desist letters from a company called Acacia Research Corporation. Acacia claimed to hold five patents on streaming video technology and dozens of other patents. Acacia doesn't actually produce any technology from its patents but instead files suit to collect fees whenever any of its patents is infringed upon. Because of the high price of patent litigation, most organizations when faced with a patent suit simply pay the patent holder in order to license the troll's patent. Although technically this business technique is legal, many have equated the practice to extortion. One company, Intellectual Ventures, has purchased thousands of formerly unprofitable patents, but curiously, as of late 2006 it had not filed a single patent suit. Many believe, however, that the company is positioning itself for a flurry of patent troll litigation.

Jerome Lemelson, a lone "hobby inventor" who obtained patents in the 1950s on everything from toys to computer vision technology, has earned hundreds of millions of dollars by threatening to sue automobile manufacturers for infringement on his patents on intermittent windshield wipers. Japan's leading car companies alone have paid millions to Lemelson to settle out of court. He successfully defended his patent right as inventor of Hot Wheels toy cars, which he patented before anybody knew what a Hot Wheels car was.

Many see a patent as the road to riches, incorrectly judging the importance of their invention. There are many websites that focus on these strange and unusual patents. Enter "silly patents" into Google to see some of these, or go to http://totallyabsurd.com. Many of the seven million patents granted in the United States consist of nonviable ideas. So patents accumulate. A great many useless and silly ideas surround the rare nuggets of accomplishment.

Patent History

The U.S. government issued its first three patents in 1790. Samuel Hopkins received the first one on July 31 for a process for making potash. George Washington signed it. Potash is an impure form of potassium carbonate. It is used to make soap, glass, fertilizers, and gunpowder. It is a very important substance and was the country's first industrial chemical.

During the mid-eighteenth century potash making became an American cottage industry. Colonists used the burned-out ashes from wood fires and leached them in iron kettles, then boiled the liquid and created a potash distillate. For a while, our forest-rich land supplied not only our own potash needs but those of England as well, but early Americans could hardly keep burning trees just to get at their ashes.

Hopkins used a furnace to reburn ashes. His process greatly improved the yield of potash as well as its purity. For the next seventy years America was the world's main potash producer. Finally, in the 1860s, German chemists showed how to mine potassium salts from dry alkali lake beds. The wood-based potash industry ended soon afterward. The world doesn't get the potassium salts it needs from wood anymore. But for a long time, Hopkins had put the United States at the center of a great chemical process industry.

The first patent in America was not a federal patent. It was granted by Massachusetts in 1641 to Samuel Winslow for a process for manufacturing salt. As previously mentioned, the first U.S. patent was issued on July 31, 1790, to Samuel Hopkins for his process of making potash. In the first year of the U.S. system, Thomas Jefferson, the first patent commissioner, granted just three patents. In 1836 a fire destroyed all the patents issued from 1790 till then, 9,957 patents. These first patents were not numbered but arranged alphabetically by the inventor's name. Less than 3,000 of these patents were recovered from various sources and then reissued. These first patents are called the X patents because they were reissued with an X to distinguish them from the numbered patents. Numbered patents began with number 1 on July 13, 1836. Patent number 1 was granted to J. Ruggles for notched train wheels.

Before a classification system was devised, patents were arranged alphabetically by the inventor's name and kept in makeshift file boxes. Jefferson insisted that patents be arranged in such a way that they could be researched easily, so patents were kept in wooden shoe boxes, and this became the standard filing system. A visitor to the Patent and Trademark Office in Crystal City, Virginia, can still see the millions of U.S. patents shelved in metal and wooden "shoes."

Few people are aware that during the Civil War, the Confederacy had its own patent office headed by former Union patent examiner Rufus Rhodes. The

Confederacy's first patent was issued on August 1, 1861, to James Houten for a breech-loading gun, and the last Confederate patent, number 266, was issued on December 17, 1864, to W. Smith for a percussion cap rammer. Understandably, many of the Confederate patents were for war machines. The Confederate Patent Office was destroyed during the battle for Richmond in April 1865, and virtually all of the models and records were lost, although some still exist in scattered private collections.

By the late twentieth century, the U.S. Patent and Trademark Office was an anachronism in that virtually the entire patenting process, from application to searching for existing patents, was still performed manually. Recently patents and drawings have been automated, and the chapter in this book on patent searching shows ways in which a patent search can be done online by librarians. However, the traditional method of storing and searching patents on paper is still in use.

From the first patent to the seven millionth one issued, the Patent and Trademark Office has had a difficult time managing the patenting process. In the last twenty years the debate over these difficulties has grown heated. Although the PTO has poured hundreds of millions of dollars into modernizing what was once a manual, paper-intensive process, issues still remain as to what exactly constitutes a patent, software's ability to be patented, the shortage of patent examiners, and the rise in patents that are held by foreigners.

It has not been a simple task to automate, digitize, and bring up-to-date the huge number of patents and their accompanying documentation. Not only do more than seven million patents have to be categorized and shelved, but hundreds of thousands of patent applications are submitted annually, and hundreds of thousands of associated documents must be controlled. It is important that the Patent and Trademark Office retain all of these records, which are indispensable in case of an infringement suit.

In the last decade the Patent and Trademark Office has embarked on a billion-dollar project to automate the system. Some searching procedures have been automated, and private vendors, including Google, have made computerized databases of patents available. The PTO itself makes a great number of patents available online at www.uspto.gov. The chapter on patent searching in this book explains how to search for a patent using online resources.

Successful Patents

One indication that the old manual filing system worked—at least for simple inventions—is that over the past 200 years no other country can show a better record of innovation than the United States. There is still a widespread belief that a patent on a simple invention will make an individual rich and secure for the rest of his life. One example of such a simple device is the snooze button on alarm clocks, which was patented in the 1950s and is included in virtually all alarm clocks sold today. The reality is quite different, but sometimes this dream of wealth from a simple patented invention can come true.

Play-Doh, the plastic modeling compound with the distinctive smell, was originally an attempt at creating a wallpaper cleaner. Joe McVicker, who was employed by Kutol Chemical in Cincinnati in 1955, saw the potential for the product as modeling clay after he gave his sister-in-law, a nursery school teacher, samples of the product for her class. The product was a great hit because it was pliable instantly, unlike other clays that had to be worked a long time, and it dried out, allowing creations to remain permanent. McVicker sold the idea to Rainbow Crafts. That company was responsible for marketing the clay as Play-Doh, introducing the distinctive yellow container and marketing the product in multicolored four-packs. Before his twenty-seventh birthday McVicker became a millionaire. Interestingly, a patent was not granted on Play-Doh until 1964, patent number 3,167,440.

A simple invention very familiar to librarians is the disposable ballpoint pen. A Hungarian journalist named Laszlo Biro invented the first ballpoint pen in 1938. Biro had noticed that the ink used in newspaper printing dried quickly, leaving the paper dry and smudge-free. However, the thick ink would not flow from a regular fountain pen. Biro fit a pen with a tiny ball bearing in its tip. As the pen moved along the paper, the ball rotated, picking up ink from the ink cartridge and leaving it on the paper. This principle of the ballpoint pen actually dates back to an 1888 patent owned by John J. Loud for a product to mark leather, but the invention was never marketed to the general public and was obviously overlooked when Biro applied for a patent. Biro first patented his pen in Hungary in 1938 and applied for a fresh patent in Argentina in 1943 after emigrating there. The press hailed the success of this writing tool because the pen could write for a year without refilling, and it became a fad in the United States. *Biro* is still the generic name used for the ballpoint pen in most of the world. Nevertheless, the pen leaked, skipped, and often failed to write. The ballpoint pen fad ended due to consumer unhappiness, and Biro neglected to get a U.S. patent for his pen.

In 1945 Marcel Bich, a French baron and production manager for a French ink manufacturer, and his partner Edouard Buffard bought a factory near Paris to manufacture parts for fountain pens and mechanical lead pencils. Bich saw enormous potential for an inexpensive, high-quality ballpoint pen that didn't skip or leak. Bich obtained patent rights to the pen invented by Biro, altered the patent, and began to manufacture simple, reliable, affordable pens in 1950. He named the company Bic after his own name in a nod to Biro, who had named his pen after himself. The highly popular modern version of Laszlo Biro's pen, the BIC Crystal, now has a daily worldwide sales figure of fourteen million pieces. In 2005 Bic sold its one hundred billionth pen.

However, a brilliant invention may be useless without the technology to make it practical. Alexander Graham Bell's telephone (patent 174,465) required the additional inventions of switching devices, amplifiers, transformers, and transmission mechanisms. A new company may need to be started once certain large patents are granted in order to obtain the capital support, management skill, and technical expertise needed to make a truly great invention successful. Bell's invention, for example, gave birth to the Bell Telephone Company.

The preceding anecdotes and examples give a librarian background on several of the important foundations of the patent system. But the question asked of librarians most often is how one obtains a patent. The first step in the application process is to search existing patents to ensure that a patent has not already been issued for one's invention. Instruction on how to do this online is outlined in the next chapter.

How Much Does a Patent Cost?

A lot depends on how complex the patent is, what technology is used (chemical patents are more expensive than mechanical patents), the number of existing patents that need to be searched, the fees of the patent attorney, and the location of the patent attorney. Attorneys in large metropolitan areas tend to charge more than those in smaller communities.

The basic fees charged by the Patent and Trademark Office amount to $1,200, which includes a filing and examination fee. This is the lowest cost possible, even if an individual files a patent entirely on their own without the assistance of a patent attorney or patent draftsperson to make the drawings. This fee includes three patent claims, the technical wording as to what precisely is being patented. Additional claims will cost more.

Problems with the patent application would lead to additional fees for appeals and legal assistance, and these costs mount quickly. A single appeal costs between $500 and $1,000, depending on its complexity.

Drawings made by a patent draftsperson cost between $75 and $200 per sheet, depending, again, on the complexity of the invention. The final patent must include drawings made to PTO specifications.

Attorney fees vary greatly. The national average for a patent attorney is about $250 per hour. In Boston the average is $325 per hour.

A pre-application patent search, described in the next chapter, costs $500 to $1,000 if done by an attorney. A patentability opinion by a patent attorney regarding the viability of the inventor's invention ranges from $500 to $1,000.

So the cost to obtain a patent can range from $1,200 at rock bottom to $5,000 for a minimally complex application using an attorney, and from $10,000 for a moderately complex invention to $20,000 for a complex invention. In some cases a very complex invention with legal assistance and appeals and professional drawings can run well over $20,000.

Questions and Answers about Patents

Q   What cannot be patented?

A   Discoveries, scientific theories, technical notation of scientific truths or mathematical methods, purely aesthetic creations (covered by copyright), combining two patented devices, naturally occurring plants, naturally occurring genes.

Q If an invention has been patented by somebody else and the patent has expired, can you get a patent on it yourself?

A No. You cannot get a patent on anything that has been previously patented. Also, you cannot get a patent on anything shown in a magazine or any other publication anywhere in the world, whether it is patented or not. Legally, this is called "anticipation."

Q Twenty years ago you invented something but never applied for a patent. You find out that somebody else has recently patented your invention. Do you have any rights to the invention, if you can prove the date of your invention?

A No. The delay in patenting your invention defeats your rights.

Q Is filing an application not recommended because others can see, copy, or steal your invention by going to the PTO and looking at the filed applications?

A No. Applications are filed in secrecy by law. Outsiders have no access to patent information.

Q Inventors often mail themselves a drawing and description of their invention by certified mail. Is this a good way to protect your rights as an inventor?

A No. Certified mailers are poor substitutes for a signed disclosure by a witness that is submitted to the PTO.

Q You invent a can opener. Your uncle gives you money to finance the manufacture of the can opener, so you file the patent application in both your names. Can you do this?

A No. Patent applications have to be filed in the name of the true inventor(s). If non-inventors are named in the application, it may invalidate the patent.

Q You file an application for a patent and find out after mailing your application that the invention already exists. Are you liable as an infringer?

A No. Manufacture, sale, or use is infringement. An application is not an infringement.

Q If you see an invention that is patented in Spain, can you get the U.S. patent on it?

A No. Only the true inventor has the right to patent in other countries. Also, the publication of a patent in Spain would come under anticipation laws (see above).

Q Something you have invented appears in the drawings of somebody else's patent, but no mention is made of your invention in that patent's claims. If you manufacture the invention shown but not mentioned in that patent, are you liable?

A No. Only the claims of a patent determine infringement.

Three

Searching Patents

The first step in the process of applying for a patent is to search existing patents to ensure that a patent has not already been issued for one's own invention. When performing a patent search online, the primary thing to bear in mind is this: web pages change frequently. There are a number of illustrations in this book that show how the web page appears. The Web being the Web, however, the look of the actual page may have changed by the time this book is in print. Even if this occurs (and it does frequently with the PTO website), the graphics may not be the same or the position of the link may have changed, but the information that is supposed to be on the page is there somewhere. Every effort has been made to ensure that the illustrations of web pages in this book are the most recent ones available.

A decade ago, the patent-searching process was a manual process. Patents were held at the U.S. Patent and Trademark Office's Public Search Room in Crystal City, Virginia, or at dozens of Patent and Trademark Depository Libraries (PTDLs) scattered throughout the United States. At the PTO Public Search Room, patents were in the form of paper booklets arranged in subject areas, called classes. Each class fit into one or more wooden "shoes"—shelving divided into small boxes. Once a searcher had identified which class to search, she went to that shoe, pulled the booklets, and leafed through an entire classification. The disadvantage was that one had to be in Virginia to do this search.

The location of Patent and Trademark Depository Libraries was usually more convenient. PTDLs are primarily public and academic libraries scattered across the United States that hold at least a twenty-year backfile of U.S. patents. The disadvantage to performing a manual search at a PTDL was that, except for a few libraries, the patents were stored on reels of microfilm in numerical order.

Since a patent search is done by identifying a subject area, called a class, the patent numbers within a class may be varied. In order to do the search, a searcher had to first get a list of patent numbers in a given class and then find the correct reel of microfilm with one of the patent numbers in the class and view it. Other patent numbers within the same class might be on dozens of different reels of film. Each reel had to be located, loaded into a film reader, and scrolled to the correct number. In addition, if a copy of a patent was needed, the film had to be copied frame by frame. This was a very time-consuming and sometimes expensive way to search patents.

In the last decade the PTO has embarked on a billion-dollar project to automate the search process. Existing patents were digitally scanned and loaded into a database that is available on the Web. This process removed the two great disadvantages to the search room process and the PTDL process—geography and lack of class order, respectively. The disadvantage that remains is that not all patents have been loaded into the database. Before 1975, access to full patent records is not always available on the Web. To the amateur searcher this may not seem to be a great disadvantage, since a patent is only in effect for twenty years. But once a patent has been issued, even if its term of protection has expired, it may not be patented again, so a complete patent search would necessarily have to cover all patents and not just the last twenty years of patents.

This chapter will cover the web-based patent search and not the manual search process. The web-based search may be completed anywhere with web access and a knowledge of the process. The step-by-step procedure explained here is a method that can be used by librarians in assisting amateur searchers through the complicated process of patent searching. The searcher or librarian need not read all the steps before proceeding but may perform the steps as they progress through the search. By following the steps in order, the patent search proceeds rapidly and eliminates unnecessary legal and technical explanations that often confuse an inexperienced searcher.

Librarians often need to assist amateur inventors who want to search a patent themselves before deciding whether to invest the money to hire an attorney and continue to pursue a patent. One obstacle is the complexity of the U.S. Patent Classification System, which contains over 400 major classifications and 108,000 subclassifications.

The web-based patent-searching procedure presented below divides the search into two major areas: locating the field of search and determining prior art. *Field of search* gets its name from the fact that it assists the searcher in determining which "field" or subject area in the vast classification system a patent is most likely to be classified in. This process of determining the relevant class/subclass areas is like a librarian's attempt to find the call number in order to locate a book.

Once the relevant field of search has been identified, prior art is the process of actually viewing "prior" or previously patented inventions in those designated classifications. *Art* to the Patent and Trademark Office is a term for any technology. So prior art guides the searcher in locating existing patents in a related subject area that may be similar to the invention being searched.

STEP 1: Identify the Parts of the Invention

In a web-based patent search, a necessary part of the search involves the identification and listing of an invention's major components. A component is a device that by itself could be patented. It is a widely held conception that a patent is awarded for a single device. In reality a patent is a combination of many things combined to create a single invention. It is rare today to find an invention that is made from only one device or that can be described with only one term.

For example, an invention such as a flashlight that powers itself by means of a small electric generator that is operated by turning a handle would not only be identified by the term *flashlight* but also by the components that may play a role in the functioning of the flashlight, such as generator, crank, hand-powered devices, lamp, lightbulb, illumination, and so on. Terms for components help to get to the synonyms for the invention being searched.

Often a searcher's thinking is too narrowly focused. If a searcher were looking for the patent on what is marketed as a Hula Hoop, only the trademark Hula Hoop comes to mind, but more terms for the components that make up the invention can be identified if the searcher is aware of the technology that makes the hoop work. Generally it may be described as a toy, so this becomes a searchable term.

Occasionally an invention is so simple that however the searcher tries to describe its components, only one or two words come to mind, and indeed some simple inventions have no common name. An example of this is the jar opener. The type of jar opener used for this example is shown in figure 3-1.

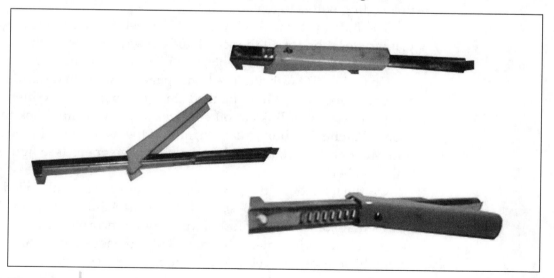

Figure 3-1

Jar opener

How would this invention be described? The searcher should think of broad synonyms that may be used to describe the invention. In this example the term *opener* comes to mind and should be included in a list of component terms to search. *Jar* is another term, as is *vise*, since, as the picture suggests, this type of opener is really a simple handheld vise. If the searcher thinks very broadly, this device is really a simple hand tool, so *tool* may be a keyword, although a very broadly defined keyword. Other terms may be *can opener* and *bottle opener* because their relationship to the same application—opening a container—may lead the searcher to a classification that includes all types of devices to be used in opening closed containers.

These terms that a searcher thinks of in describing the components of an invention are called keywords. It is important that a searcher be armed with as many keywords as possible before proceeding, even if the words are only marginally related to the invention being searched. It is very important that a searcher keep a record of what terms were identified! It is a good idea to create a word-processing document in which will be kept all the notes made during the search process. If later in the process a searcher decides to seek professional legal advice, these records will help keep the patent attorney from duplicating the work already completed. The collected and recorded keywords are then searched in the Index to the U.S. Patent Classification (we will refer to this work as "the Index"). In Step 2, the searcher consults the Index to assist in more specifically describing the invention.

STEP 2: Consult the Index to the U.S. Patent Classification

The Index is necessary in locating the patent subject areas, called classifications, which categorize an invention. The searcher must have these classifications before proceeding with a patent search.

The Index is located within the PTO website, www.uspto.gov. This site is the primary location for all the search aids described during the search process and is the source for the actual patents, including text and images.

Go to the PTO website. The home page is shown in figure 3-2. Bear in mind that the page's look may have changed since this book was written. On the left side of the page is a list of links to other pages in the website. Click the link that has the word "Patents." A box will open, and in the list of links in the box select "Guides and Manuals." Click that link and a new page opens (see figure 3-3). There's a lot going on here.

On the left side of the page, near the bottom, is a link called "Guidance, Tools, and Manuals" (see figure 3-4). Click it. The disclaimer at the top of the resulting page warns that some of the information may be incorrect. One thing to bear in mind when working with patents is that patenting is not static. Changes are frequent. This is one benefit of the web-based system—changes can be made quickly. Changes were formerly printed in the Index only once a year, in December, when the Index existed only in paper.

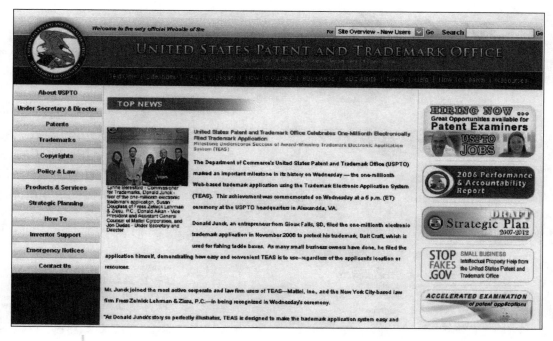

Figure 3-2

Home page of the PTO website

The page that is displayed by clicking the "Guidance, Tools, and Manuals" link has two major sections, "Patents Guidance" and "Tools and Manuals." Under "Tools and Manuals" is a subheading called "Classification" and under that one called "U.S. Patent Classification (USPC) Index." Click on "U.S. Patent Classification (USPC) Index." The page that is displayed is shown in figure 3-5. The searcher has two options, the Index in HTML format or the Index in PDF format. The PDF format is a duplication of the paper Index, and many more keywords can be viewed in it at one time; however, the HTML format contains links to patent definitions, which are explained below, so this one will be the format used.

At this point the differences between a manual and an automated search become evident. While the web-based search allows for up-to-date information that is readily available without regard to physical location, the negative side is the Byzantine process of explaining to a novice how to conduct the search. A librarian just a decade ago would have explained how to find the Index by giving a call number. By contrast, just explaining how to locate the Index online takes five procedures.

By using the Index to look up the keywords identified in Step 1, a searcher can get the classification of the invention being searched. The Index contains keywords arranged in alphabetical order. Beneath each word is a more specific description. To the right of each word are two columns of numbers. The first is the major classification, and the second is a subclassification. For clarification of this step, the jar opener will be used as an example of a patented device being sought.

United States Patent and Trademark Office

Home | Site Index | Search | FAQ | Glossary | Guides | Contacts | eBusiness | eBiz alerts | News | Help

Patents

Check NEWS & NOTICES for the latest Patent news, announcements and official notices

Patenting ...

Basic facts about patents
How to get a patent ⚡
Types of patents
Registered patent attorneys & agents ✉

You can APPLY for a patent online *(EFS-Web)* ✉

Accelerated Examination

Corresponding re: patenting *(rules for)*
see
  • Responding to office actions (§700)
  • Customer-requested actions (all)
  • Assignment ⊞ of ownership (§300)
    >> *more* about assignments
Manual of Patent Examining Procedure - *MPEP* ⊞

FEES and payments $
Look-up & Pay Patent Maintenance Fees $

FORMS - printable & fillable ▥

Mailing Addresses ⚡

Patent Appeals & Interferences - procedures &
proceedings ⊞
(Board of Patent Appeals and Interferences)

Patent Prosecution Highway (JPO/USPTO fast-track
examination):

if either the Japan Patent Office (JPO) or the USPTO rules that at least
one claim in an application is patentable, an applicant may request that
the other office fast track the examination of corresponding claims in
corresponding applications

Patent Publication Services

SEARCH ✉ existing patents and published applications

See eBusiness column on right for patent searches;
assignment ⊞ searches & services; e-filing; application status
& images of documents; and more online services.

Guides ...

⚡ **About Patents, Trademarks, Servicemarks and**
Copyrights
⚡ **Guidance, tools & manuals**
  ▪ **Policy & procedures**
  Advanced users: also see Patent Examination Policy
  ▪ **Special patent mailboxes**
⚡ **Training & conferences**

eBusiness
What you can do online ...

Use **Patent Electronic**
Business Center ✉
to file, search, check status, view
documents, and more...

Help ...

⚡ **FAQ** - questions & answers
▪ **Glossary**
⚡ **How to search patents & more**
⚡ **Inventor Assistance Center**
⚡ **Inventor Resources** - Basics for new inventors
  Musicians, Artists & Authors
▪ **Patents Organization Chart** (org chart, advanced
resources & phones)
⚡ **PCT Help** (international patenting)

Search Aids ...

✉ **Patents OG (eOG:P)** – browse recent weeks' patents
▪ **OG (Official Gazette)** – regular & special notices
▪ **Manual of Patent Classification** – search tip - after
retrieving a class listing, click the ▣ icon for any class in the online
manual to automatically search and retrieve patents for that
classification code
▪ **Search Templates** describe search resources for the
classified areas of science and technology found in the USPTO
Manual of Classification. The templates provide more structure to the
search activity and set a standard to measure the completeness of
any search.

See **How to Search** *for more search tools and tips*

▪ **Plugins and viewers**
  - **PDF, TIFF patent images**, etc.

⚡ **PTDL - depository libraries** for patent and trademark
information and general research assistance

▪ **Authority file** – list of Patent Numbers in the online Image
database
▪ **Expired patents**
▪ **Extended Patent Terms**
▪ **Patent numbers** (ranges for each year)
▪ **Statistics, weekly data & lists**
▪ **Withdrawn patents**

Resources ...

Figure 3-3 PTO website's "Patents" page

United States Patent and Trademark Office   PATENTS

Home|Site Index|Search|FAQ|Glossary|Guides|Contacts|eBusiness|eBiz alerts|News|Help

Patents > Guidance, Tools & Manuals

WARNING: The information which follows was correct at the time of original publication. Some information may no longer be applicable. For example, amendments may have been made to the rules of practice since the original date of a publication, there may have been a change in any fees indicated, and certain references to publications may no longer be valid. Wherever there is a reference to a statute or rule, please check carefully whether the statute or rule in force at the date of publication of the advice has since been amended.

Patents Guidance

- Proposed Rule Changes to Focus the Patent Process in the 21st Century
- Notices: Recent Patent-Related *pre-OG, OG & Federal Register*
- Access to Published Patent Applications
- Application Data Sheet (ADS) Guide
- Business Methods Patents
- Disclosure Document Program
- Examination Guidelines for Computer-Related Inventions &
  - Training Materials
- General Information Concerning Patents
- General Information about 35 U.S.C. § 161 Plant Patents
- Guide to Filing a Utility Patent Application
- Guide to Filing a Design Patent Application
- International Guidance
- Revised Interim Utility Guidelines Training Materials (1999) [PDF]
- Office of Patent Publication
- Patent Business Goals (PBG) Final Rule Home Page
- American Inventors Protection Act of 1999 (AIPA) Home Page
- Provisional Application for Patent brochure
- Restriction Practice - TC1600
  - Training Materials- TC1600
- Revised Interim Written Description Guidelines Training Materials [PDF]

Tools & Manuals

- Classification:
  - Concordance, U.S. Patent Classification (USPC) to International Patent Classification (IPC) Eighth Edition
  - Cross-Reference for Nanotechnology
  - Examiner Handbook to the US Patent Classification System
  - Manual of Patent Classification
  - U.S. Patent Classification (USPC) Index
- Forms
- Manual of Patent Examining Procedure
- Patent Laws, Consolidated [PDF]
- Patent Rules, Consolidated [PDF]
- Search Templates

Some contents linked to on this page require a plug-in for **PDF File.**

KEY: =online business system $=fees =forms =help =laws/regulations =definition (glossary)

The Inventors Assistance Center is available to help you on patent matters.Send questions about USPTO programs and services to the USPTO Contact Center (UCC). You can suggest USPTO webpages or material you would like featured on this section by E-mail to the webmaster@uspto.gov. While we cannot promise to accommodate all requests, your suggestions will be considered and may lead to other improvements on the website.

Figure 3-4

"Guidance, Tools, and Manuals" page

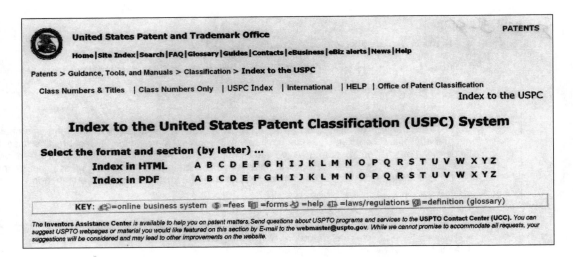

PATENTS

United States Patent and Trademark Office

Home | Site Index | Search | FAQ | Glossary | Guides | Contacts | eBusiness | eBiz alerts | News | Help

Patents > Guidance, Tools, and Manuals > Classification > Index to the USPC

Class Numbers & Titles | Class Numbers Only | USPC Index | International | HELP | Office of Patent Classification

Index to the USPC

Index to the United States Patent Classification (USPC) System

Select the format and section (by letter) ...

Index in HTML   A B C D E F G H I J K L M N O P Q R S T U V W X Y Z
Index in PDF   A B C D E F G H I J K L M N O P Q R S T U V W X Y Z

KEY: ✎=online business system   💲=fees   📄=forms   ✍=help   ⚖=laws/regulations   📖=definition (glossary)

The Inventors Assistance Center is available to help you on patent matters. Send questions about USPTO programs and services to the USPTO Contact Center (UCC). You can suggest USPTO webpages or material you would like featured on this section by E-mail to the webmaster@uspto.gov. While we cannot promise to accommodate all requests, your suggestions will be considered and may lead to other improvements on the website.

Figure 3-5

"Index to the U.S. Patent Classification" page

In Step 1 a searcher would have broken down this device into its parts and listed any synonyms that might also describe the device. The components/synonyms would be *jar, opener, can, vice, cap, lid,* and any other term that comes to mind that describes either the thing itself or the components that make up the jar opener. The goal is to look under as many of these synonyms and related words as possible in order to obtain as many access points to the Index as possible. It is better to have too many terms than not enough, since some terms will not appear in the Index.

The listing for "Jars" in the Index is shown in table 3-1. There is a lot of information contained in this short listing. The "See Pot" reference means that there is a separate listing in the Index alphabetically under "Pot" and that some things called "jars" will be listed there. The indented terms list the various types of jars that are classified in the system, and all other types of jars are listed under "Pot." The first column of numbers gives the major patent classification. The second column, after the slash, contains the subclassification.

The invention being searched, jar opener, is not listed here, but this is not a dead end. The "see" reference gives the searcher another category. The searcher would refer to "Pot" in the Index.

But before going to the "Pot" listing in the index, what exactly is "Fruit jar vises," and is this important, since "vise" was one of the keywords identified in Step 1?

Table 3-1

Index listing for "Jars"

Jars See Pot	
Acid proof	206 / 524.1+
Battery	429 / 164+
Design	D09
Drilling rig part	175 / 293+
Fruit jar vises	81 / 3.31+
Leyden	361 / 301.1+
Receptacle	215
Support	211 / 74+
Support associated with funnel	141 / 328
Wide mouth	D09 / 516+

STEP 3: Consult the Patent Definitions

If a searcher comes across a word or phrase in the Index that confuses him, the PTO has provided a dictionary of sorts to the words used in the Index. It is called the "patent definitions." Before the Internet, these patent definitions were kept in a notebook at the PTO and were copied to microfiche that was then distributed to the PTDLs. The quirk of the old paper/microfiche definitions was that patent examiners would sometimes make corrections to the notebook by penciling changes, deletions, and additions, and these handwritten notes appeared on the fiche. Now the changes are made to the database as they occur.

To locate the definitions and to see if they can answer the question of what is a "Fruit jar vise," a searcher has to find the specific web page containing that definition. To make web navigation easier, all directions to a web page from here on will be done with shorthand. The home page or start page will be listed, then the link to click, preceded by an angle bracket. For example, to get to the page that has the definitions: **www.uspto.gov > Patents > Guides and Manuals > Guidance, Tools, and Manuals > Manual of Patent Classification.** You should be at the point shown in figure 3-6.

Admittedly this is the longer method of locating a patent definition. One of the advantages of using a web-based searching method is that at times there is more than one way to accomplish the same thing. The shorter method, since the HTML format of the Index is being used, is to simply click the class or subclass numbers listed to the right of the term in the Index. This will lead to a brief descriptive phrase of what the term means, and if a longer definition is needed, the searcher again clicks the class number on the brief phrase page. Links to click at this stage

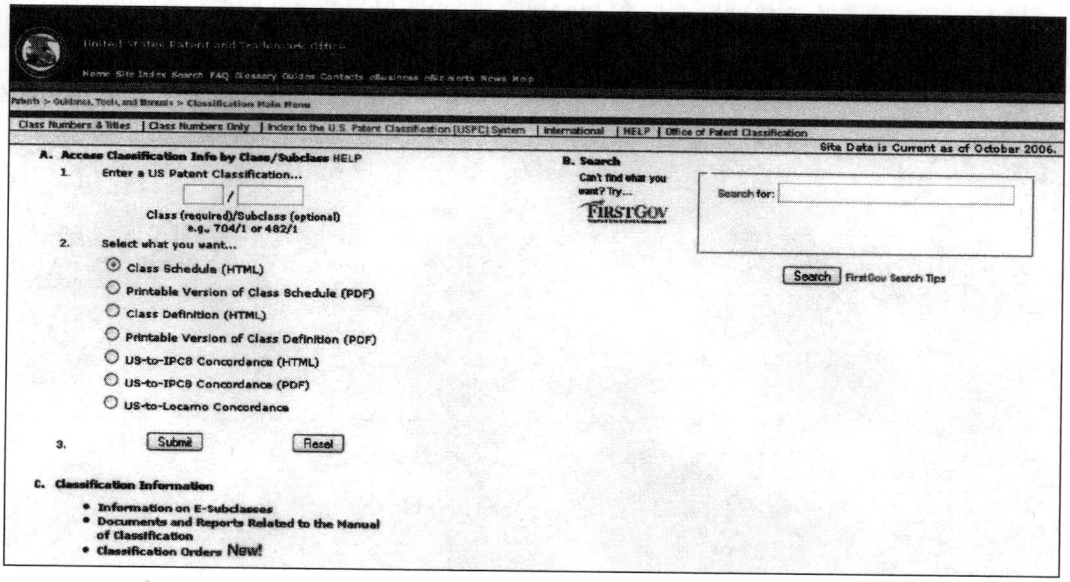

Figure 3-6

"Class/Subclass" page

of the search can be identified by the blue-colored text, while the rest of the text is in black.

In the black boxes at the top, fill in the class and subclass number listed beside "Fruit jar vises" from the Index—81/3.31. Do not enter the + symbol; this will be explained later. Click the radio button that reads "Class Schedule (HTML)" and click "Submit."

The text that you will see is shown in table 3-2. Bear in mind that these definitions are written by lawyers and patent examiners and so are not in simple language. But by reading the definition, one understands that a fruit jar vise is a device that holds the jar while a separate tool is used to remove the lid. The opener shown does not have a separate vise but is handheld while the opener is applied to the lid. The searcher should bear in mind that this definition is of the subclass and not the class. To see what class this fruit jar vise fits in, simply click the class number 81 in the Index beside the term "Fruit jar vise." Class 81 is the class that is defined as "Tools." Table 3-3 shows how this class is defined.

This short definition tells the searcher that the tools categorized in this class are not limited to any "art." In patent language "art" means a technology. For example, all ovens are not categorized in one class but are categorized by their technology. Gas ovens will be in one class because their "art" is gas. Electric ovens will be in a separate class, and wood-fired ovens are in another class. So then the tools in

Table 3-2

A patent definition

3.31   With receptacle supporting or grasping means: This subclass is indented under subclass 3.25. Removers combined with means to support and/or grasp the receptacle.

  (1) Note. Removers having structure which engages the receptacle during removal of the closure but does not support or grasp the receptacle are excluded.

  (2) Note. This subclass and the indented subclass include receptacle holding or grasping means, per se, as well as in combination with closure engaging means.

  (3) Note. For can openers having receptacle supports, see Class 30, Cutlery, subclasses 436, 447 and 448.

SEE OR SEARCH CLASS:

269   Work Holders, appropriate subclasses. Class 269 is the residual locus for patents to a device for clamping, supporting and/or holding an article (or articles) in position to be operated on or treated. See notes thereunder for other related loci.

Table 3-3

Class 81 definition

CLASS 81   TOOLS

SECTION I - CLASS DEFINITION

In this class are tools which are not structurally limited to any classified art.

This class is limited to hand tools, except in the subclasses noted in Subclass References to the Current Class, below.

---

class 81 are tools that can be used in a variety of technologies. The other thing this definition tells the searcher is that the tools in class 81 are hand tools and not power tools or large stationary tools like a lathe. But there are exceptions, and those exceptions are listed if one reads further down in the definition text.

The Symbols

Before looking further, the searcher should learn the meanings of the symbols that accompany the numbers in the columns to the right in the Index (table 3-1). Knowing their function will save time and make the process easier to interpret.

Patent classes are numbered rather than described with words. The "D" in front of some of these class numbers means that this type of patent is a design patent. When most people think of a patent they think of a utility patent. A design patent is protection on the design of something rather than protection of the device itself. For example, a chair may be supported by four legs, a pedestal, or metal tubing, or it may be shaped in some unusual way. In securing protection for these variations, a chair designer does not reinvent the chair, since the chair's function has not changed, but makes the chair appear differently. That is, the chair itself cannot be patented, but the critical feature of design in it can be patented. This design would be protected by a design patent. If the searcher is not seeking protection for a design but for a unique device, the classifications preceded by a "D" may be disregarded even if the words describing the design class seem to be appropriate.

The second column of numbers may contain a plus sign (+), asterisk (*), or decimal numbers. The plus sign and the asterisk will be explained in Step 4 as the searcher learns about the organization of the Manual of Classification, but a mention of the decimals in the subclass column can be done here. Their origin gives some insight into the history of the PTO and the problems of organizing over seven million documents.

The History of Classification

The U.S. Patent Classification System was developed in the nineteenth century. Originally it was structured by having class 1, 2, 3, and so on. This part of the classification remains unchanged today, with over 400 class numbers. If new major classifications were needed, they were simply added at the end. However, subclass numbers within each classification are arranged by technology. For example, machinery that operated on electricity would always be subclassed between subclasses 10 and 15 in a particular classification. A problem arose as new technologies were developed. Subclasses 10 through 15 were filled with particular types of electric machines, and then a totally new group of electrical inventions came along that necessitated their own classification, but subclasses 10 through 15 were already being used. The PTO could not simply add numbers at the end of the subclass sequence because the arrangement was according to technology. That is, electric patents had to fit somewhere between 10 and 15 unless the PTO rearranged the entire Patent Classification System.

The solution was that a suffix was added to the subclass number. New electric technologies would be classified as 10A, for example. That worked fine for a while, until the PTO ran out of letters in the alphabet. It then added two-letter prefixes like 10AA or 10AB. As more and more patents were added, the classification scheme got complicated, and it was possible that a subclass might eventually need to be followed by twenty-six letters. The final solution was to add subclassifications with a decimal, such as 10.1 or 10.22. The decimal solution is used today, and each number seen is a unique subclassification.

Returning to the Search

Since looking under "Jars" in the Index proved fruitless, the searcher should use the "see" reference and look in the Index under "Pot." Go to the Index again and this time look for "Pot": **www.uspto.gov > Patents > Guides and Manuals > Guidance, Tools, and Manuals > U.S. Patent Classification (USPC) Index.** As shown in table 3-4, there are several other "see" references here.

Table 3-4

Index listing for "Pot"

Pot (See Bowl; Jar; Kettle; Pan)	
Burner	431 / 331+
Chamber	4 / 479+
Coffee	99 / 279+
Coffee or teapot strainers	210 / 473+
Receptacle spout attached	210 / 466+
Cooking container	D07 / 354+
Dash (see dashpot)	
Fire pot thermostats	236 / 104
Flower	47 / 65.5
Design	D11 / 143+
Furnace and metallurgical	
Fire pot	126 / 144+
Fire pot thermostats	236 / 104
Glue pot heater	126 / 284
Material heating furnaces	432 / 156+
Material heating holders	432 / 252+
Metal melting and casting	164 / 335+
Solder pot heater	126 / 240
Glue heating	126 / 284
Holder	16 / 435+
Open top liquid heating vessel	126 / 373.1+
Railway rail supports	238 / 110+
Railway signals	246 / 475
Vulcanizing	425 / 283

Note that listed under "Pot" are subcategories ranging alphabetically from "Burner" to "Vulcanizing," and most of these subcategories, like "Furnace and metallurgical," have their own subcategories. Look down the list to see if there is any wording that would describe the jar opener. Nothing here is even remotely associated with a can or jar opener. Now what? More "see" references mean that new words are added to the keyword list—"Bowl," "Kettle," and "Pan," but these seem to be leading the search in a different direction. It isn't the type of container that is being sought but the means to open its lid. Each keyword in the list that was created in Step 1 should be located in the Index in an effort to find a class and subclass that best describes the opener pictured before diverting off into "see" reference areas. The next keyword is "Opener."

Go to the Index, and under "Opener" is the listing shown in table 3-5.

Look down the list of subheadings under "Opener and Opening Device." There is a listing for "Can or bottle" opener. The class number, however, is preceded by a "D," and as was explained earlier, this class relates to the appearance of the opener and not to its function. It is the patent on the function of the opener that is being sought, so this class can be disregarded.

Table 3-5

Index listing for "Opener"

Opener and Opening Device	
Bag opening	493 / 309+
Closing combined	493 / 255+
Cutting closing combined	493 / 199+
Refolding combined	493 / 244+
Web forming cutting closing	493 / 199
X-art	493 / 963*
Bottle or jar	
Cap	215 / 295+
Stopper in combination	215 / 228
Stopper removal facilitated	215 / 295+
Can cutter	30 / 400+
Closure opener combined	7 / 152+
Combined	7 / 152+
Can or bottle	D08 / 33
Closure metallic receptacle	220 / 260
Closure remover	81 / 3.07+
Combined	7 / 151+
Pliers combined	7 / 126+
Envelope	83 / 912*
Cutters	30 / 233
Inkwell pen actuated	15 / 257.075
Oyster	452 / 13+
Paper	
Bag with tear strip	383 / 200+
Box with tear strip	229 / 200+
Carton or box	30 / 2
Envelope with tear strip	229 / 307+
Parachute	244 / 149
Railway coupling knuckle	213 / 115+
Textile fiber	19 / 80 R+
Wood box	408 / 53

Since this is a fairly long list of keywords, is there any way to help decide which of these terms may be relevant without having to look at the definitions of each? If the searcher reviews the list of keywords created in Step 1, the broadest keyword to describe the jar opener was "Tool." Earlier in this section, when we were learning to locate patent class and subclass definitions, the definition of class 81 was shown. This is the general class for handheld tools that apply to no art.

The opener shown in figure 3-1 can be used to open bottles, jars, or any receptacle with a screw on top, and it is a hand tool. That would put it in class 81. If a searcher looks again at the Index shown in table 3-5 for "Opener and Opening Device," is there something listed that falls into class 81? There is. It is described in the Index as a "Closure remover" and is shown in class 81 subclass 3.07+.

An experienced searcher would have located this right away because a professional searcher usually searches only a handful of classifications in which he is expert, and he would know that class 81 would be the most obvious place to find a handheld opener.

This is not the end of the Index search. Each term that was listed in Step 1 must be located in the Index, if possible. The reason that the search is continued is that patents do not carry just one class and subclass. Inventions are classed in several different areas that relate to individual components, and all possible classifications must be located before moving on to the next step. The Manual of Classification in the next step and the use of patent definitions in a later step will both give many classifications to search in locating a particular invention. When the searcher is finished with Step 3, he should be armed with a handful of patent class and subclass numbers.

STEP 4: Consult the Manual of Classification

The first three steps of the patent search were explained using the Index to the U.S. Patent Classification. Before beginning Step 4, the patent searcher should have several possible classifications (class and subclass numbers) that relate to a particular invention. The patent shorthand for writing class and subclass numbers is 81/3.07+, for example, using the class and subclass located in Step 3. Even if a searcher is reasonably sure that a single correct classification has been found, all related classifications and subclassifications should be explored because a patent is not placed in one classification but in several. One of these is identified as the primary classification and related classes. There is no strict rule as to which classification is the primary class. Patent examiners often just pick one as the primary class.

The Manual of Classification is the beginning point of Step 4. A decade ago, the Manual was a two-volume set of three-ring loose-leaf binders. Now, blessedly, the Manual is online. In the Manual, each classification is given one or more pages. The subclassification numbers are listed in two columns on each page and include a two- or three-word description of each subclassification.

In Step 2 a jar opener was used to help explain the use of the Index, and it was determined that it was most likely to be placed in class 81, a class titled "Tools." The searcher should locate 81/3.07+ in the Manual. Go to **www.uspto .gov > Patents > Guides and Manuals > Guidance, Tools, and Manuals > Manual of Patent Classification.** The page should look like that shown in figure 3-6 earlier. Enter the class and subclass numbers in the box at the top. Do not include the +. Click the radio button that reads "Class Schedule (HTML)" and click the "Submit" button.

Table 3-6 shows part of class 81 as it is printed in the Manual. Since this is only a partial listing of what appears in the Manual, it is a good idea at this point to look in the online Manual for the full listing to get a sense of how the terms are related and organized.

Table 3-6 Class 81 schedule

Class	81	TOOLS
2		COMBINED WRENCHES AND PUMPS OR OILERS
3.05		SHELL, PROJECTILE, OR WAD EXTRACTORS
3.07		RECEPTACLE CLOSURE REMOVER
3.08		· Having discrete retainer or receptacle for removed closure
3.09		· Combined or plural
3.15		·· Attached to receptacle or closure
3.2		· Power-, vacuum-, or fluid pressure-operated
3.25		· Wall or surface mounted or supported
3.31		·· With receptacle supporting or grasping means
3.32		··· With bottom support
3.33		·· Rotary remover device, gear or lever actuated
3.27		·· Lever or prying type
3.35		· Movable into or over handle
3.36		· With additional receptacle-engaging means
3.37		·· Lever- or gear-translated closure remover
3.29		·· For engaging receptacle about closure (e.g., socket type)
3.39		·· Bottom support
3.4		· Gripping type
3.41		·· Finger grapple type
3.42		·· With reciprocating closure-engaging
3.43		·· With deformable strip-tightening means
3.44		·· With pivoted closure-engaging parts
3.45		· Screw type
3.55		· Levering or prying type
3.47		·· With impaling or inserting remover
3.56		·· Having discrete relatively movable portions
3.57		·· Having handle, intermediate hook, and end fulcrum
3.48		· Impaling or inserting type
3.49		·· With lateral projection or abutment
3.5		SPECTACLE

As explained previously, subclasses are arranged by technology and not numerically or alphabetically. In some subclass listings it may seem that the arrangement is numerical, but on closer inspection it will become clear that some class numbers are not listed in order. This can be seen in table 3-6, where subclass 3.45 is followed by 3.55 and then 3.47. The subclass is sometimes taken out of order and placed elsewhere in the subclass listing. If a subclass is not listed in its logical place—for example, subclass 43 does not come between subclasses 42 and 44—look through the subclass listing for it. It will be there—unless it has been changed to another classification. Before we narrow down the search area even further by using the Manual, a brief digression to explain the symbols encountered in the Manual is useful. Following this explanation is a further exercise to reduce the number of possible class/subclasses that will have to be searched.

The Symbols

The symbols are explained here in Step 4 because although they appear in the Index in Step 3, their meanings cannot be interpreted without some introduction to what they refer to in the Manual.

Table 3-7 shows an example of the keyword "Harness" in the Index. "Harness/Body/Design" is listed as class D29 subclass 101.1+. Obviously this is a design patent in class 29, but the plus sign after the subclass number is puzzling.

In table 3-8, which is a facsimile from the Manual, notice how some of the subclasses of class 54 are in all caps and how some are indented under another term. Those capitalized are the first subdivisions of the class; for example, subclass 24, "Halters," is an immediate subdivision of class 54, "Harness." Those listings that are preceded by dots are further subdivisions of those listings that are uppercase; for example, subclass 6.2, "With halter," is a subdivision of "Bridle," which is a subdivision of "Harness." Those listings with two dots preceding them are subdivisions of those listings with one dot, and so on.

Class D29 subclass 101.1+ shown in the Index example for "Harness" (see table 3-7) means that a searcher should look not only at D29/101.1 but at everything that has dots under 101.1 in the Manual until the next uppercase listing is reached.

For example, if the Index had told the searcher to search 54/6.1+, the searcher would have to search 54/6.1, 54/6.2, 54/7, 54/8, and 54/9 through 54/15 because they are all preceded by dots. The search

Table 3-7

Index listing for "Harness"

Harness (See Body, Harness)	54
Animal stocks	119 / 729+
Body	
Design	D29 / 101.1+
Fire escape	182 / 3+
Land vehicle occupant	280 / 290
Parachute	244 / 151 R
Bridles	54 / 6.1+
Buckles	24 / 164+
Design	D30 / 139
Checking devices	54 / 70
Collars	54 / 19.1+
Design	D30 / 134+
Feed bags supported by	119 / 67
Hames	54 / 25+
Hand package carrier	294 / 157+
Loom	139 / 82+
Drawing in warp	28 / 203.1+
Hand pushed	139 / 30+
Motions for dobby looms	139 / 66 R+
Pads	54 / 65+
Saddles	54 / 38.1+
Stirrups	54 / 47+
Trunk	190 / 27
Protecting	190 / 26

Table 3-8

Class 54 schedule

Class 54 HARNESS FOR WORKING ANIMAL	
71	BREAKING AND TRAINING DEVICES
72	· Leg spreaders
77	OX YOKES
2	TRACK
3	YOKES
24	HALTERS
85	· Connectors
6.1	BRIDLE
6.2	· With halter
7	· Bits
8	·· Mouthpieces
9	··· Double
10	· Blinds
11	·· Covering and uncovering
12	· Brow bands
13	· Crown loops
14	· Gag runners
15	· Stranglers
57	UNDERCHECKS
16	CHECKREINS
17	· Hook loops
61	CHECKHOOKS
62	· Movable keeper
70	CHECKING AND UNCHECKING DEVICES
35	MARTINGALES
36	REINS
74	REIN HOLDS
63	TERRETS
73	REIN GUARDS

would continue until the next uppercase listing was reached. If the searcher skips Step 4, those additional classifications would be missed.

The asterisks (*) seen in some class/subclass listings in the Index are added to the subclass listings more as a benefit to the patent examiner than to the patent searcher, but an understanding of this symbol will aid the searcher in understanding the structure of the classification system.

The asterisk is an indication of what the PTO calls a "cross-reference art collection." This has nothing to do with paintings or sculpture. An art collection, to the PTO, is a collection of patents relating to a particular technology, or art. For example, as was stated earlier, ovens may be gas, electric, or wood-fired or fueled by other methods. Because the subclasses are arranged by technology, each type of oven would be placed in a subclass that relates to the technology it uses. A patent examiner searching for oven patents would have a difficult time locating all of the appropriate subclasses, so to make it easier the examiner creates an art collection. Art collections are digests set up by patent examiners, but they are also official subclasses. Art collections contain only examples of oven patents that are placed in the digest by patent examiners to represent the variety of technologies that ovens use to produce heat. When an examiner is considering an oven patent, the art collection acts as an index pointing to other classifications where oven patents reside. A searcher can use the art collection in the same way to cross-reference an existing patent to several classification areas.

The "DIG" abbreviation in the Index stands for "digest." A digest is the same as a cross-reference art collection except that it is not an official subclass. It acts as an informal index to other related patents.

Table 3-9 is an example from the Index that has a lot going on in it. It shows a design class, D07, a subclass 323, a plus sign indicating that there are subcategories of this subclass that should be searched, and a DIG symbol as a subclass of class 53. The title of class 53, which a searcher would learn from consulting the Manual, is "Packaging." "Packaging" is also the keyword that the Index uses to describe the types of patents that belong in class 53. The DIG means that patents in this group, 53/DIG 1, are patents that relate to just the packaging of hot dogs. The reason they are assigned a DIG category is that an examiner has placed a representative

Table 3-9

Index listing for "Hot Dog"

Hot Dog	
Cooker	D07 / 323+
Packaging	53 / DIG 1

sample of hot dog packaging patents here to aid in a search where many different subclasses need to be searched. A DIG subclass may contain only one patent.

The Rationale of the Manual

A searcher might ask at this point why it is necessary to consult the Manual at all, since the class/subclass numbers were already given in the Index. Is there anything learned in Step 4 that wasn't already learned in Steps 2 and 3? Yes.

In Step 3 the searcher progressed to the point where there was a good indication that what the PTO called a "closure remover" was the jar opener the searcher was seeking. But there was no verification of that. If the Manual showed that a "closure remover" was listed under buttoning devices rather than under openers, the searcher would know that it was a dead end. Without this verification from the Manual, the searcher would waste time searching an unrelated group of patents.

Another reason to use the Manual is that keywords are listed in the Index without regard to definition, so it is often unclear what the listing means. Table 3-10 shows the Index listing for "Fly."

What is a "Closer lasting tool"? Could it be some esoteric term for a fly swatter? To find out, a searcher would consult class 12/113 in the Manual and see that a closer lasting tool is grouped with other patents relating to the manufacture of shoes. By using only the Index this information is not clear. The Index and the Manual should be used together in a patent search.

Table 3-10

Index listing for "Fly"

Fly	
Brush	416 / 501*
Closer lasting tool	12 / 113
Fishing	43 / 42.24+
Design	D22 / 125+
Holders for fishhooks, flies	43 / 57.1+
Net	54 / 80.4
Paper box making	493 / 52+
Swatter	43 / 137
Design	D22 / 124
Textile spinning	57 / 96
Trap	43 / 122

Back to the Manual

If left with just the class/subclass listing 81/3.07+ a searcher is going to have quite a few class/subclass listings to search. The listing for 81/3.07+ from the Manual is shown again in table 3-11.

As was explained earlier, 81/3.07+ means to search subclass 3.07 and everything that is indented below it until the next listing in uppercase letters is reached. In this example, that means that 81/3.07 through 81/3.49 would have to be searched. That's twenty-seven different subclasses with, at times, hundreds of patents in each subclass. By using the patent definitions and an understanding of the basic function of the type of opener that is being searched, many of these subclasses can be eliminated. This makes the next step, searching the actual patents that appear in a subclass, much easier.

Table 3-11
Class 81 schedule

Class	81	TOOLS
2		COMBINED WRENCHES AND PUMPS OR OILERS
3.05		SHELL, PROJECTILE, OR WAD EXTRACTORS
3.07		RECEPTACLE CLOSURE REMOVER
3.08		• Having discrete retainer or receptacle for removed closure
3.09		• Combined or plural
3.15		•• Attached to receptacle or closure
3.2		• Power-, vacuum-, or fluid pressure-operated
3.25		• Wall or surface mounted or supported
3.31		•• With receptacle supporting or grasping means
3.32		••• With bottom support
3.33		•• Rotary remover device, gear or lever actuated
3.27		•• Lever or prying type
3.35		• Movable into or over handle
3.36		• With additional receptacle-engaging means
3.37		•• Lever- or gear-translated closure remover
3.29		•• For engaging receptacle about closure (e.g., socket type)
3.39		•• Bottom support
3.4		• Gripping type
3.41		•• Finger grapple type
3.42		•• With reciprocating closure-engaging
3.43		•• With deformable strip-tightening means
3.44		•• With pivoted closure-engaging parts
3.45		• Screw type
3.55		• Levering or prying type
3.47		•• With impaling or inserting remover
3.56		•• Having discrete relatively movable portions
3.57		•• Having handle, intermediate hook, and end fulcrum
3.48		• Impaling or inserting type
3.49		•• With lateral projection or abutment
3.5		SPECTACLE
3.6		• Plier
3.7		LEAF-SPRING SPREADERS
3.8		FUSE PULLERS
4		ENGRAVERS' CLAMPS

Look at the picture of the opener again in figure 3-1. How does this jar opener work? Before moving on to each subclass, define the jar opener's design and operation in order to try and identify terms that may be of use when looking at the subclass list in the Manual. This opener would be explained, for example, as a tool comprising two channeled pieces of steel or some other durable material such as plastic. One channeled piece fits into the other to allow the top piece to slide along the bottom piece. Each piece is slotted to allow a stop along the surface that makes adjustment to various sizes of caps possible. When the correct adjustment is made for the size of the cap, the top piece pivots in a simple lever-type method downward, and a tooth in the top piece engages a given slot in the bottom piece to secure the cap. Jaws on both pieces grip either side of the cap. When secure the tool is rotated to remove the cap.

Look at the section of the Manual again in table 3-11: 3.07 is the general subclass, and the next indented listing is subclass 3.08, which is identified as "Having discrete retainer or receptacle for removed closure." If the wording is confusing, click the subclass number (on the Manual subclass link, hold the "Control" key while clicking) and get a definition. This phrase is saying that devices in subclass 3.08 have a receptacle for the cap. Does the jar opener in question have a container to hold the removed cap? No. Then this subclass can be disregarded. The definition for subclass 3.09 is for an opener that is combined with another tool to remove caps. The invention in question is a single tool, so this subclass too can be eliminated.

The searcher should look at each subclass. If uncertain as to its relevance, do not eliminate it. Only eliminate the subclasses that are certainly not related to the invention in question. For example, "Power-, vacuum-, or fluid pressure-operated" would be eliminated, but "Lever or prying type" and "With pivoted closure-engaging parts" would not be eliminated, since in the detailed description of the tool above, the words *lever* and *pivot* are terms that were used in the description. Again, if unsure of the terminology, click the definitions, and if still unsure, do not eliminate the subclass for the next step.

STEP 5: Get a List of Patents in Each Class/Subclass Group

Previous steps in the search process have guided the patent searcher through the steps that make up what is called the field of search. The field of search identifies the proper classifications in which to locate a particular patent. The field of search, even for an experienced searcher, is confusing and carries with it the potential for mistakes. After completing the field of search, the searcher is armed with a listing of possible class/subclass areas to search in order to begin the prior art search. Prior art identifies patents in the designated classifications and leads to actual viewing of patent documents. Prior art is easier in some ways than field of search but is more time-consuming.

Something should be said here about the importance of a prior art search and the amount of time that an amateur searcher should reasonably spend on it. A searcher makes a search to verify that an invention is not already patented. There is no penalty for submitting an application to the Patent and Trademark Office for a device that is already patented, but the money spent on making the application and preparing the drawings and the time spent on preparing the application will be lost if the PTO finds that a patent already exists for the invention being submitted.

There are some inventors who are willing to risk an application without performing a search at all, although the PTO requires that a listing of class/subclass groups searched be included on the patent application. This is not as bizarre as it sounds. Even though an amateur searcher or an attorney has performed what is considered a comprehensive search, the PTO performs its own search. If the PTO finds an existing patent, the applicant will also lose all fees. An inventor must weigh the potential risk of losing the application fees against the time and money he is willing to spend on searching prior patents.

Keeping Records and Attorney Fees

Before beginning the viewing of patents, the searcher should keep accurate records of what has been searched. Many searchers will complete the field of search, the subclass list, and a partial viewing of patents on their own but will hire an attorney to interpret certain complicated patents or to complete the search of patents in a subclass list. The attorney will want a record of what has been done up to that point. If the record is not complete and accurate, the attorney will duplicate the search already done at their per-hour charge, which defeats the purpose of performing a search by oneself.

The fees for hiring legal assistance vary depending on the law firm and whether the attorney handles the entire process from start to finish or performs only selected services. A full patent search and application can cost $15,000 or more, but typical costs average $5,000. The cost of a pre-application patent search by an attorney is typically in the range of $500 to $1,000, so doing the search on one's own can save a significant amount of money. In all cases the attorney should be a registered patent attorney. These lawyers are required to pass an examination given by the PTO to certify that they may practice patent law. These patent attorneys can be found by going to the home page of the PTO, www.uspto.gov, and clicking on the "eBusiness" link at the top of the page and selecting the "Registered Patent Attorney or Agent" link under the "Patents" area.

Patent agents may also perform patent searches and file patent applications. A patent agent must pass the same written test as a patent attorney and must also have a specified amount of professional training in engineering. The difference is that a patent agent is not a lawyer. An agent is trained in patent law and procedures but has not passed the bar exam.

What to Do with a Subclass List

Before going any further, the searcher will have to download software that will enable a given computer to view the TIFF-formatted text and drawings that make up a patent document. To do this, go to www.uspto.gov and click the "eBusiness" link at the top of the page. The resulting page is separated into three areas: "Patents," "Trademarks," and "Other." Under the "Patents" section there is a clickable link called "Search." Under that link is, in blue text, a link labeled "How to View Patent Images."

The resulting page will give instructions on how to download the software and how to view the patent images, so that will not be explained here. The AlternaTIFF software is recommended, if that software is compatible with the computer and browser being used to search patents. When loading the software, make sure that the computer (e.g., PC or Mac) and the browser (e.g., Internet Explorer, Netscape, or Firefox) that will be used are selected when configuring the software. If this is not done, the patent text and images will not be viewable or only partial images will download. If the searcher has set up the software to work with Netscape and then uses Internet Explorer as their browser, again the images will not download.

Officially, the subclass list is called the Classification Sequence—Subclass Listing, or the U.S. Patent Classification—Subclass Listing. For the sake of brevity, here it will be called the Subclass List.

The best introduction to the Subclass List is to view it online. There are several ways to get the Subclass List—the list of patents in a given class/subclass. The simplest method is, while viewing the hierarchy of patent subclasses in the Manual as was done in the last step, to click on the red "P" that appears at the far left beside each patent subclass number. A list of the patent numbers in that subclass will be displayed.

Another method is to go to **www.uspto.gov > Patents > Search > Advanced Search** and in the box marked "Query" type "ccl/" plus the class/subclass being sought. For example, if seeking class/subclass 81/3.07, type "ccl/81/3.07" in the query box. By using the query box, patents can be searched in a variety of ways, such as inventor name, words in the patent abstract, and so on. The proper method to search these areas is given by clicking the text. In this example, since a subclass list is being sought, only that method is detailed here. There are dozens of ways to use the advanced search to locate patents, and another entire chapter of this book could be used to explain the value of the advanced search and its flexibility in locating patents.

In the "Select Years" box under the query box, the searcher has the option of searching only the years 1976 to the present or 1790 to the present by using the drop-down menu. From 1976 to the present contains full-text patents with images. Prior to 1976, only patent images and/or brief descriptive information are available. If unsure whether the patent being sought would be possible before 1976, select 1790 to the present. Since the invention being sought is a simple manual jar opener that could have been invented in 1900 or 1999, 1790 to the present should be selected.

In the last step, by using detailed descriptive terms to describe the jar opener, several possible class/subclass pairs were selected. In describing the invention the words *steel, plastic, channel, slide, slotted, pivot, lever, jaws,* and *rotated* were all used. The class/subclass pairs in the range 81/3.07 to 81/3.49 should be examined in both the brief descriptive phrase next to the subclass number in the Manual and in the more detailed patent definitions. The class/subclass pairs should be those whose description contains the initial keywords selected in Step 1 and the words used in the detailed description of the patent being sought. Already eliminated are 3.08, which is an opener with a receptacle for the removed cap, and 3.09, which is a combined jar opener, but 3.33 should be included since the short descriptive phrase includes both the terms *rotary* and *lever*. Subclasses 3.27, 3.37, 3.44, and 3.55 all mention *lever* or *pivot* and should be included.

In actual practice, all listings of patents for all of these subclasses would be viewed. Each patent in each subclass would be included if it came close to describing or looking like the patent being searched. This is the part of a patent search that takes the most time. Table 3-12 shows the listing of patents when the searcher views subclass 3.44, for example.

STEP 6: Eliminate Unrelated Patents

A searcher should know how to eliminate patents that are not related to the invention being searched. This part of the search requires some skill and familiarity with the technology that created the invention being searched. Being able to view a patent and make a decision quickly on its relationship to another invention is a valuable skill.

Some patents can be eliminated by the title. In the subclass list above for 81/3.44, the patent titled "Anti-fraud lock screw with a freely rotating dome on

Table 3-12

Patent listing for Class 81 subclass 3.44

PAT. NO.		Title
1	7,051,621	Gripping device
2	6,971,282	Container opener
3	6,918,150	Combined nutcracker and bottle opener
4	6,860,177	Anti-fraud lock screw with a freely rotating dome on a polygonal head
5	6,854,361	Jar opener
6	6,736,030	Champagne cork remover
7	6,679,138	Bottle opener
8	6,263,761	Pill bottle opener
9	6,257,091	Automatic decapper
10	6,189,421	Slip nut wrench
11	6,142,039	Bottle cap remover
12	6,035,508	Vacuum seal releaser and method
13	6,019,018	Grind stone removing wrench and method of using same
14	5,943,920	Jar and bottle lid closing and opening device
15	5,862,720	Bottle opening tool
16	5,655,806	Tongs with tapered jaws
17	5,595,094	Oil filter wrench
18	5,546,831	Gripping system for rotary objects
19	5,528,961	Ice bucket champagne opener
20	5,347,889	Multi-purpose wine bottle stopper device
21	5,275,070	Device for removing wine bottle stopper
22	5,249,488	Oil filter remover
23	5,161,435	Container seal removal apparatus
24	5,083,482	Lid wrench
25	5,065,648	Oil filter wrench
26	5,031,485	Container lid opener
27	5,027,678	Cam actuator means with connector assembly
28	5,000,063	Bottle stopper puller
29	4,995,295	Lid wrench
30	4,970,917	Stud extractor and wrench apparatus
31	4,964,330	Oil filter accessory
32	4,949,576	Self-adjusting lid wrench
33	4,932,544	Bottle holder
34	4,919,015	Screw cap opener
35	4,914,985	Radiator cap removing tool

a polygonal head" is a much more complicated opener than the one being sought, but the patent right below it titled "Jar opener" cannot be eliminated by title alone. A word of warning: even though the anti-fraud lock screw seems like a candidate for elimination at this point, the searcher should at least look at the drawing of the invention. A complicated patent may incorporate as one of its components a device that is based on a simple invention and therefore may be related to one's own invention. The deciding factor if the searcher sees in a complicated invention a part that may look like a more simple invention being sought is to look at the part of the patent called the "claims." These are explained below.

The searcher should ask: "What is it about my particular jar opener that makes it unique and patentable? Is it made with a unique design?" If there are several unique things about an invention, the searcher should focus on one item at a time until he gets the hang of searching. The jar opener being searched has one unique thing about it—the two parts of the opener slide along each other to adjust for various cap sizes and then lock in place at the desired adjustment. This then is the focus of the search.

Amateur searchers have one advantage over professional patent searchers. The amateur searcher is likely also the inventor of the device. The unique features of an invention are well known to the inventor, and since the inventor is working with one particular technology, that technology is very familiar to him. For example, the inventor of the jar opener knows what features make it adjustable. When the amateur searcher is going through class 81/3.44, it is readily apparent whether an existing patent has the unique features of the new invention.

Patent attorneys usually do not search the patents at the PTO themselves. They hire professional searchers in the Washington, D.C., area to perform searches for them. These professionals search a wide spectrum of classifications. Although these professional searchers are very good at what they do, they didn't invent the jar opener and must depend on documentation from the patent attorney who hires them or on communication with the patent attorney to explain what is unique about the patent being searched. The amateur is usually quicker and more aware of subtleties in existing patents.

Let's assume that the amateur has followed all the steps described so far and has identified a class, has a list of patent numbers, and has eliminated a number of patents that seemed unrelated. Just what is it in the patent that a searcher is looking for? There are two primary items: the drawings and the claims.

STEP 7:   Consult the Claims to Eliminate Unrelated Patents

Claims are the effective part of a patent. They are numbered paragraphs that give a precise description of the invention and list all essential features that are being "claimed" as unique. The claims are the basis for a patent infringement suit in that what is unique about an invention must be mentioned in the claims. Claims are located in the patent text immediately following the statement "What I (we) claim is:" and each claim is numbered.

In disclosing a patent (that is, publishing the patent complete with drawings, descriptions, claims, etc., as is done when a patent is granted), occasionally some unique feature is not claimed although it appears in the drawings. Patent experts maintain that one may copy an unclaimed part of the invention without liability, since it is not described in the claims. So it is important that every unique feature of an invention be accurately described in the claims.

Claims define the structure of an invention in precise terms. The legal protection given the patent is delineated by the claims and not the drawings, disclosure, specifications, or any other part of the patent. Patent attorneys and agents are trained in the art of writing a claim narrow enough to show uniqueness but broad enough to give an inventor some protection against other similar inventions. The importance of the claims cannot be overstated.

So what does this mean to a patent searcher, and how can it help in the search process? In the jar opener example used throughout this series, the answer to the question "What is unique about this particular jar opener?" can be found in the claims. In the last step it was determined that one of the unique things about the jar opener invention being searched was that it had two channeled pieces that slid along each other to allow for size adjustment. In the viewing of the actual patent, a searcher could look at the drawings to see if an existing jar opener patent had adjustment, and if it did, the searcher could read the claim to see if it adjusted by the same method. The variations can be extensive. For example, do the adjustment pieces nest within each other, do they lock when adjustment is reached, and do they lock by fitting a pin into a slot? A searcher may make a determination for himself but cannot depend on a librarian to make that determination for him.

A great deal of care must be taken by librarians in explaining patent claims. Interpretation of claims gets into the fuzzy area of patent law, and a decision as to whether a particular claim is an infringement on an existing patent is a matter best left to patent attorneys and agents. Not only is this wise, but interpreting claims in other than a very broad explanatory sense constitutes the practice of law. Librarians and others assisting with a patent search must be careful to explain what the claims are, not interpret them. Medical librarians are familiar with this concept, since they cannot diagnose an illness for a library user or recommend treatment.

The following are the claims in patent 2,931,258. This is one of the patents in the subclass list for 81/3.44. This patent for an "opener for screw caps," granted in 1960, is one of hundreds of patents in classes 81/3.27, 3.37, 3.44, and 3.55 that the searcher would view.

What I claim is:

1. A wrench for screw caps comprising an elongated twisting bar formed to provide, a depending jaw at its front end, a handle at its rear end, and a channel-shaped intermediate section including depending side flanges and a connecting web portion, said web portion defining a row of longitudinally spaced abutment forming teeth; and a relatively short channel-shaped clamping lever including laterally spaced depending side flanges and a connecting web portion and nestingly slidably received over said twisting bar, the side flanges of said clamping lever adjacent the forward end thereof extending below the lower edges of the adjacent side flanges of the twisting bar and defining laterally spaced jaw members in generally opposed relationship to the jaw carried by said twisting bar, the forward edges of said jaw members defining gripping teeth which project forwardly of the forward extremities of the web portion of said clamping lever, a depending locking lug defined by the front of the web portion of said clamping lever and selectively engageable with a given one of the teeth defined by the web portion of said twisting bar, the rear end portions of said jaw members being inturned to define stop lugs engageable with the side flanges of said twisting bar, the spacing between said stop lugs and said twisting bar side flanges being such as to permit raising and lowering movements of the front end portion of said clamping lever with respect to said twisting bar for selective engagement of said locking lug with a given one of said abutment forming teeth but limiting upward swinging movements of the rear end of said clamping lever with respect to said twisting bar.

2. The structure defined in claim 1 in further combination with means limiting rearward sliding movement of said clamping lever with respect to said twisting bar, said means including an upstanding ear on the web portion of said twisting bar intermediate said abutment forming teeth and said handle and engageable with the depending locking lug on the front end portion of said clamping lever only in the extreme retracted position of said lever.

3. The structure defined in claim 1 in which the jaw associated with said twisting bar is formed to provide a pair of laterally spaced jaw elements, one each of which is in opposed relationship to one of the jaw members of said clamping lever, engagement of said jaw elements and jaw members limiting forward sliding movement of said clamping lever with respect to said twisting bar, and in further combination with means limiting rearward sliding movement of said clamping lever with respect to said twisting bar.

4. The structure defined in claim 3 in which said gripping teeth underlie the side flanges of said twisting bar and limit upward movement of the forward end of said clamping lever with respect to said twisting bar when said clamping lever is in substantially parallel relationship with the twisting bar, whereby to prevent accidental disengagement of said locking lug with a selected one of said abutment forming teeth.

In claim 1 the patentee's statement includes most of the significant words used to describe this particular jar opener. When the searcher sees this, he should immediately take a look at the drawings that accompany the patent. Patent 2,931,258 has just one drawing. It clearly shows an adjustable nesting channel with slots. (See figure 3-7.)

The searcher can shout "Eureka" at this point, but no decision can be made by a librarian as to this patent's significance. The searcher is also wise not to make a definite judgment at this point, unless doing the search independently without any professional legal assistance. This patent should be placed in a group of questionable patents that will be generated during the search. This group of questionable patents should then be taken to a patent attorney or agent for an interpretation. In addition, when the patent text is viewed, the text will show other patents that were consulted in the course of the search for that patent. These patents should also be viewed and their class/subclass numbers noted as possible patents or classes that have been overlooked. The important thing to remember for the librarian who may be helping a patent searcher, however, is that no interpretation can be made. That is, if asked by the searcher if the librarian feels that this patent is related or unrelated to the jar opener being searched, no answer can be given. It is up to the searcher or his attorney to make that decision.

At this point in the search process, the librarian should let the searcher proceed on his own. Interpretations, writing the patent, filing forms, and making drawings are things that are best left to the inventor and his legal representative.

An amateur patent searcher will leave the library having completed the search process and will have a small group of patents that will be shown to an attorney for interpretation.

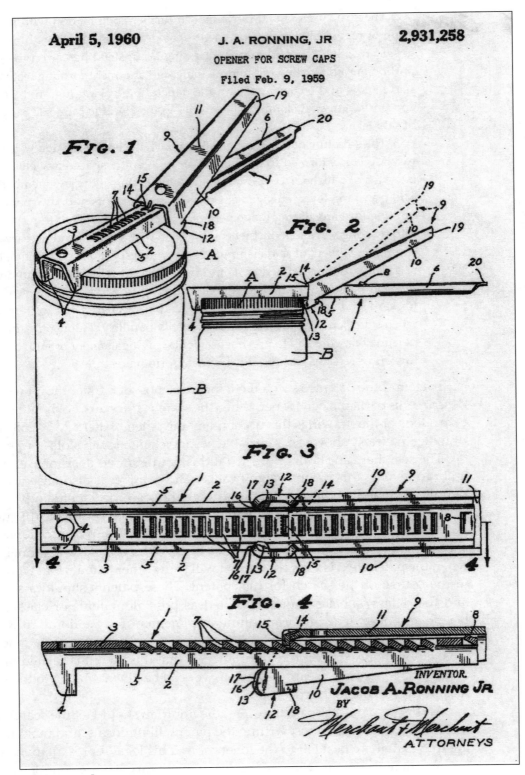

Figure 3-7 Patent drawing for the jar opener

Summary of the Process

The major steps to searching a patent are as follows:

Identify the parts of the invention. Break the invention down. For example, a generator-driven electric light for a bicycle would include a light, a generator, and a bicycle. Think of as many synonyms or related terms as possible to identify the parts of the invention.

Consult the Index to the U.S. Patent Classification. The keyword Index will give a class and subclass for each term identified in Step 1. When done with this step, a searcher will have many sets of class/subclass numbers.

Consult the patent definitions. The wording in the Index and Manual is sometimes vague. This leads to some confusion as to whether the classifications the searcher has identified are correct. The patent definitions specifically state what type of device fits into every class and subclass. This is sometimes as confusing as the Index and Manual themselves, so it's good to know that many times this step can be skipped if the searcher is fairly certain that he has the right classes.

Consult the Manual of Classification. The Manual will show the relation of the invention to other inventions within the same technology. It also provides the searcher with finer indexing of specific aspects of the invention, leading to more direct class/subclass listings.

Get a list of patents in each class/subclass group. Once the classifications are identified, the list of patents in each class can be generated.

Eliminate unrelated patents. This is done by scanning a listing of titles to eliminate obviously unrelated inventions or by using a Patent and Trademark Depository Library to view patents on film.

Consult the claims to eliminate unrelated patents. Claims state specifically what is new about the invention. By reading the claims, most patents can be kept or disregarded as unrelated to the invention being searched. Those patents that are of questionable relationship to the patent being searched should be collected and a decision made as to their relevance by the searcher himself or a patent attorney or agent.

One comfort in all of this is the knowledge that the Patent and Trademark Office will perform its own search to verify that a patent does not already exist. The searcher is going through this process because if the PTO does find a patent that the searcher has overlooked, the inventor will forfeit all application, preparation, and legal fees. As said before, the search should not cost as much in fees and the searcher's time as the inventor stands to lose if an existing patent is found by the PTO.

Step 7 in the patent-searching process completes the librarian's role in offering assistance to an amateur patent searcher. By following the steps outlined and by remembering the background knowledge presented, a librarian should be able to make a searcher feel confident and sure of the basic procedure in applying for a U.S. patent. Of course, there are many books, articles, and supplemental materials that can be pointed out to a searcher as additional aids.

Many patent writers say that the U.S. patent system has effectively eliminated the individual inventor by making the process complicated and expensive. A patent search can be an intimidating and confusing process to a novice. Clearly the system is not designed for amateurs and they are at a disadvantage, but a search can be done. Thousands of amateur searchers each year perform their own searches. Unless the invention being searched is extraordinarily complicated, such as some recent electronic devices, even those with modest educational and legal backgrounds can succeed in completing the process.

The right to patent is guaranteed by the U.S. Constitution, which wisely gave the right to individuals and not to corporations. Unfortunately, in the twenty-first century, unlike previous times when a patent on a simple idea could make an individual wealthy, it is rare today to find individuals who are able to profit from patenting a simple device. However, through its Patent and Trademark Depository Library Program and programs such as Invent America, which encourages school-aged children to invent patentable devices, the federal government is making an attempt to preserve the spirit of American ingenuity.

The U.S. patent system is a living, changing thing. The process outlined in this chapter may change in the next few years as the Patent and Trademark Office attempts to apply new technologies to make the system more user-friendly. The patent system is also not free of controversy, and in the future the PTO may change search techniques or the manner in which patents are secured. Librarians should try to be aware of these changes as they occur.

Four

Copyright

O f the three major types of intellectual property, copyright has been most affected by the digital age. Before the Internet, violation of any of the primary rights of the copyright holder was fairly obvious because the illegal copying of a film, for example, would produce a physical thing. The Internet makes it possible to copy, distribute, and display a protected film without producing a physical copy. Although some alterations to the copyright law have taken place, like the Digital Millennium Copyright Act in 1998, the law is basically that of the Copyright Revision Act of 1976, which has been in effect since 1978. Previously, as early as the player piano roll, technological changes have disrupted traditional viewpoints of copyright, and from time to time a technological breakthrough, such as the videocassette recorder, has caused changes in the interpretation of the law.

Since 1988 when the United States signed the Berne Convention, by which a group of nations standardized and agreed to respect each other's intellectual property laws, copyright is assumed upon the creation of a work. Virtually everything that is "fixed" in any medium of expression is copyrighted. This means that when a work is created and takes a physical—or digital—form, it is automatically protected by copyright. A drawing made on a napkin in a restaurant is protected by copyright. A crayon picture that a preschooler made is copyrighted.

The concept of fair use, a concept codified for the first time in the 1976 law, has been practiced for centuries in order to use copyrighted material for educational and informational purposes without first requesting permission from the copyright holder.

What Is Copyright?

Copyright is the exclusive right given by law for a certain term of years to an "author" who can be a writer, composer, designer, and so on, to print, publish, and sell copies of her original work. Fair use is using, under certain conditions, a copyrighted work without first asking permission of the owner, including reproductions for purposes such as criticism, commentary, news reporting, teaching, scholarship, and research.

Copyright applies to text, but it also applies to music, sculpture, painting, motion pictures, jewelry designs—in short, anything creative that is "fixed in a tangible medium" according to Title 17 of the U.S. Code. "Fixed in a tangible medium" means that the copyrighted item has to be written or printed on paper, carved in stone, painted on canvas, or recorded on film or videotape, for example. But in the digital age "fixed" also means existing in a digital format. Ideas are not protected by copyright, but once that idea takes a physical—or digital—form, it is copyrighted. The concept of "fixed" is important. An impromptu dance is not copyrighted, but if that dance is written on paper in choreographic notation, it is. If that dance is taped for broadcast over the Web, it is copyrighted. If a photograph of the dancer is digitized and placed on a website, it is copyrighted. A rule of thumb is that once an idea takes any fixed form, it is protected.

It is important to distinguish copyright from patents. Patents are granted on functional items of design like belt buckles or the design of a chair. Copyright is granted on items that are functionally useless. For example, a patent would protect a doorstop shaped like a book because the doorstop is a functional item; the doorstop has the function of keeping a door open. A book itself would be copyrighted because it is useless in a functional sense.

What Are the Six Rights of Copyright?

The Right to Copy

This is one of the clearer concepts of copyright law. If one creates something artistic that is fixed in some medium, only that person who holds the copyright may make a copy of the thing created. The best-known artistic creation in the area of copyright is a book. If an author writes a book, only the copyright holder can make a copy of all or part of that book. Librarians often see library users making a copy of an entire book on a photocopy machine. This is illegal under copyright law.

Suppose a person purchased an original painting. The artist who created the work holds the copyright on that painting. Who would hold the rights to make copies of the painting? The artist. Even though a person purchases a work of art, the copying rights remain with the artist. This is an important concept for museums that purchase works of art at very high prices. That purchase does not give the museum the right to copy that painting. Even if a person has an original work of art in their home that they legally purchased, they may not make copies of that work of art.

The Right to Prepare Derivative Works

The best way to explain derivative works is with some examples. A derivative work is a movie made from a book. A derivative work is a video game based on a popular movie. A derivative work is a concept that is turned into a play, like the musical *Cats* being based on the works of T. S. Eliot.

A few years ago there was a high-profile legal case involving derivative works. A movie titled *Coming to America* was released in 1988. The basis of the plot is that an African prince arrives in the United States and experiences cultural differences there. The movie was successful and grossed over $140 million before a suit was filed. The lawsuit claimed that the concept for the plot originated from a source other than the screenwriter's brain. The plaintiff, columnist Art Buchwald, contended that *Coming to America* was based on a two-page concept that he had sold to Paramount Pictures in 1983 titled *King for a Day*. Buchwald claimed that since the movie was a derivative work based on his treatment, he was entitled to a percentage of the film's net profit. In a historic lawsuit that followed, Paramount contended that although the film had grossed $140 million, it actually made no net profit, so there was no reason to pay Buchwald. Of course, the successful film had earned millions, but in the Byzantine methods of Hollywood studio accounting, no profit was shown. When the suit was settled, the way Hollywood math is done changed forever. Art Buchwald's settlement came to more than $1 million. The important point here is that the source of a derivative work is protected intellectual property no matter how small—in this case a two-page outline.

Another example of the right to prepare derivative works involved an old railroad photograph. A competition was held in Pennsylvania for a mural that would hang in the downtown area of a Pennsylvania city. The winning proposal was a semiabstract painting of a locomotive. The artist's technique was to take a clear photograph of the locomotive, digitize it, and then reduce the resolution so that the images and colors of the photograph became rectangles of color rather than a sharp image. The copyright issue here was that the photograph used to create the mural was not one that the artist took. It was a photograph taken by a professional photographer in the 1940s and was protected by copyright. The mural was a derivative work, and no permission had been granted by the photographer to use his photograph as the basis for the mural. Fortunately for the artist and the city, the infringement issue was settled amicably out of court.

The Right to Distribute Copies

This right belongs to the copyright holder even if "distributing copies" is interpreted as a teacher handing out photocopies in a classroom. In the digital world, distributing copies would also mean posting material on the Internet, since this is worldwide distribution.

In the case of *Religious Technology Center v. Netcom*, materials owned by the Church of Scientology were placed on an Internet newsgroup through a server controlled by a company called Netcom. The church wanted the materials removed on the basis of the material being proprietary to the church and not for public distribution. Netcom refused to do this. The court found that neither Netcom nor the newsgroup that posted the material had been guilty of direct infringement on the copyright, since neither party took action to make copies. The court did find that Netcom might be liable for "contributory infringement" by materially contributing to infringement by the Internet user. As it happened, the parties settled out of court, and the materials were removed without monetary damages being awarded to the church. It is important to note here that this action took place in 1995, three years before the Digital Millennium Copyright Act gave immunity to Internet service providers if they were unaware of illegal practices by their customers and before there was a clear understanding as to whether posting material on the Internet is, in reality, distribution.

The Right to Perform Works Publicly

When a play is performed for an audience, it is publicly performed. If a copyright holder allows a play to be performed by others, she is entitled to a royalty fee and control over how the work is performed. Not only do theater groups have to pay a royalty to use scripts, but normally they must return the script booklets at the conclusion of the play. Public performance is a pretty straightforward concept, but it gets muddied when a work is performed in an educational setting or over the Internet.

For example, fair use allows reading from textbooks or novels in a classroom setting. However, stage plays cannot be performed in a classroom, nor can a student perform and act a song from an opera. The difference is that the permitted performance, reading from a textbook, is a nondramatic work, while the prohibited performance, a play, is a dramatic work that is intended to be performed. Now is a good time to state what will become obvious as copyright is explained: copyright is not simple and straightforward.

In distance education more problems arise. In a classroom, fair use allows an instructor to play a videotape, play a slide show, or play a multimedia program one time without authorization from the author. But in distance education none of these activities is considered legal. By transmitting these media over a television satellite or the Web, the works are in essence being "performed publicly" and are not limited to the environment of a classroom. In some cases, performances in distance education are permitted if the delivery site is a place where people gather for educational purposes, which might be a high school classroom or an auditorium. But in distance education, the program might also be delivered into somebody's living room, and fair use does not permit that.

The Right to Display Works Publicly

In an educational setting, it may be fair use for an instructor to show a copy of a painting in an art class, but fair use disappears if the course is a distance-learning course. In a distance-learning course, the painting would be placed on a website that is accessible to everybody in the world, making it a public display and not exclusively an educational display in a classroom. If the painting appears on a website that was designed for the class, it may be used if the website is protected in such a way as to allow access only to members of the class.

The Right of Public Performance of Sound Recording by Means of Digital Audio Transmission

This additional right was added in 1995 and is not so much a new right as it is a clarification. Before downloaded digital recordings, such as the songs from iTunes or Napster, radio stations played records in a symbiotic relationship with the music recording industry. Since airplay was advertising that would draw purchasers to their music, the music industry waived all but nominal royalty payments for music played on the air. But with the advent of services such as iTunes, this relationship soured, and the music industry wanted a statute to enable the collection of royalties from music that was downloaded from services such as iTunes or Napster. This right gives the recording industry the legal path to collect royalties on such downloaded music.

Fair Use

Within the current copyright law there is a codified concept called "fair use." Fair use is a loophole in the copyright law that allows someone other than the copyright holder to copy, display, perform, and distribute copyrighted material under certain conditions without first obtaining permission. Fair use is the necessary exception to copyright protection since without it, copyright's constitutional purpose to promote learning, advance knowledge, and promote the progress of science would be useless if each time protected material was used permission would be required. The law specifically allows fair use for purposes such as criticism, news reporting, teaching, and scholarship or research. However, trying to decipher those purposes is confusing.

Fair use is the most important intellectual property concept that librarians are likely to face. Although fair use has been a part of copyright law for 200 years in the United States, it has been codified only since 1976. Before 1976, fair use evolved through a series of court decisions to arrive at a sometimes vague concept.

Fair use evolved as courts tried to balance the rights of copyright holders against society's interest in making copies of a protected work for teaching purposes. If not for fair use, every time a teacher wanted to use copyrighted material for educational purposes, permission would have to be obtained from the copyright holder. Obviously, this is not practical. Without fair use, copyright would severely limit the educational uses of *all* the materials created by others. The goal of fair use is to avoid the rigid application of the copyright statute when it would stifle the very creativity the law was meant to foster.

Fair use is a contradiction of the basic concept of copyright. Fair use provides the privilege of using an author's work without permission or payment. In 1976 the new copyright act spelled out fair use—but only with resistance. The copyright committee working on the new law felt that trying to nail down specific guidelines for fair use in an era of technological change was futile. This was prophetic, given that it was 1976 and the explosion of digital technology was still years away. However, the law was passed with fair use guidelines, and later the Digital Millennium Copyright Act and the Conference on Fair Use (CONFU) refined fair use as applied to a digital environment.

The Four Factors of Fair Use

The codification of fair use is short and seemingly straightforward in the text of the law, but this still does not make its application any clearer than in the past. Virtually anything written or available on the Internet is copyrighted. The four factors that determine fair use are spelled out in the law to help guide those who wish to utilize fair use, but it is still difficult to explain fair use because for every concept presented there is an exception. To claim fair use one must consider:

1. The *purpose* and character of the use, including whether such use is of a commercial nature or is for nonprofit educational purposes. The courts have found that the use of a copyrighted work for educational purposes is the most likely application of the fair use statute. Outside of educational purposes, any *noncommercial* use is likely to be looked upon as fair use if that use is "transformative." A work is transformative if the new work created is based on the copyrighted work but adds some new element, has a different character, or serves a different purpose. An example of this would be a parody or satire of an existing work. So a *noncommercial* parody of a song would be fair use.

2. The *nature* of the copyrighted work. The gist of this guideline lies in how the work is to be used. For example, a how-to book on woodworking contains plans that are to be copied by the reader. It is assumed that the reader is not going to take the book into the wood shop but rather photocopy the plans and use the copy in the wood shop. The physical nature of the work is significant in this guideline.

3. The *amount* and substantiality of the portion of the copyrighted work used in relation to that work as a whole. One hundred words taken from an encyclopedia for educational purposes may be fair use, but one hundred words taken from a children's book may not be. The application of this guideline is not simply in the volume of material used but in what portion of the entire work that excerpt constitutes. Even though the amount of material used may be small, if it is deemed to constitute a significant part of the whole or is substantial in terms of importance, it is not permitted. That is, even if a small amount of a short story is used, if it is considered to be the heart of the story, it is not permitted.

4. The monetary *effect* of the use upon the potential market for or value of the copyrighted work. This is perhaps the best-understood concept of fair

use. If the use of protected material significantly affects the potential of that work to provide a monetary profit to its author, the use is infringement and not fair use. In educational settings, making copies of a work for nonprofit use would be permitted under fair use if *all four* fair use guidelines were followed. If a professor uses copyrighted material for educational or nonprofit use, this does not mean that the professor need not be concerned about the amount used. A professor could not make photocopies of worksheets from a single purchased workbook for all the students in the class. This would be detrimental to the market potential of the original work.

These four factors reflect the balancing act that fair use requires. No litmus test exists for what uses would be considered fair under copyright law, but educators can feel reassured by the fact that courts award damages on the proof that actual financial loss to the copyright holder has occurred because of infringement. If no economic gain is realized by the user, even though infringement may be proven, damage awards may not be given to the copyright holder. Also important is the need to consider all four of the factors in determining fair use. Just because a protected work is used for educational purposes does not mean that a user may disregard the rights of public display or performance.

Fair Use Considerations

To assist in making decisions on whether fair use is permissible in a given situation, the list below may be helpful. This list may be used for any consideration of fair use, whether it involves digital media or other formats. The list may be considered a balance sheet in that the selection of one favorable item or one unfavorable item does not in itself permit or exclude fair use but rather weighs the pros and cons of a given situation. The final decision still rests in the hands of the educator.

Fair use would be permitted if the purpose is
- educational
- nonprofit
- news
- criticism
- parody or satire

Fair use would not be permitted if the purpose is
- commercial
- for profit
- for entertainment

Fair use would be permitted if the nature of the work is
- published
- nonfiction

Fair use would not be permitted if the nature of the work is
- unpublished

- creative (e.g., music or film)
- fiction

Fair use would be permitted if the amount used is
- small
- not central to the work

Fair use would not be permitted if the amount used is
- large
- central to the work

Fair use would be permitted if
- the work is lawfully acquired, i.e., purchased
- there is no way to obtain permission
- there are few copies available
- there is no impact on profit
- there is no similar product available

Fair use would not be permitted if
- numerous copies are made
- there is repeated use
- the profit of the copyrighted work is affected
- the work is easily licensed
- the work is available on the Internet

How Long Does a Copyright Last?

In short, copyright lasts the life of the author plus 70 years after his or her death. The current copyright law originally gave an author rights for his or her lifetime plus 50 years, but there was a 1998 amendment to that law. The Sonny Bono Copyright Term Extension Act (yes, *that* Sonny Bono) raised that limit through legislation that Bono sponsored when he was a member of Congress from California. The purpose of the extension was so that the music copyrights of certain artists of the rock-and-roll era who died young would not expire while their music was still popular. Without the adoption of the extension in 1998, the music of artists like Buddy Holly (who died in 1959) and Janis Joplin (who died in 1970) would have entered the public domain in the early twenty-first century. Before 1978, the year the Copyright Revision Act went into effect, copyright was valid for 28 years, plus renewal for 28-year periods up to a total of 95 years. Some have maintained that the Walt Disney Company used its influence to ensure that the Bono extension would pass, since the first appearance of Mickey Mouse was in 1928 and Mickey's copyright was due to expire shortly without the extension.

In the event of a work being authored anonymously, copyright lasts 95 years from the date of registration or 125 years from the date of creation, whichever is shorter. Note that since 1988 it is not required that a work of art be registered in order to claim copyright. Copyright is assumed on creation. It is also not necessary

Table 4-1

Copyright protection periods

If the work was created	The term of protection is
Before 1923	In the public domain
1923–1963	28 years plus renewal for 47 years (plus another 20 years by the Sonny Bono Act enacted in 1998) making total protection time 95 years. If not renewed, protection expired after 28 years.
1964–1977	28 years plus renewal for 67 years
1978 and after	The life of the author plus 70 years. In cases of multiple authors, the protection under the latest law (1976) is the life of the longest living author plus 70 years. In cases of anonymous works, the 1976 law protects the work for 95 years if the work is published.

to display the copyright symbol (©) on works. But if a copyright is not registered with the Copyright Office, the burden of proof to show unregistered ownership of the copyright rests with the copyright holder.

To make this issue a bit easier to determine, table 4-1 lists protection periods for works created under each copyright law.

Fair Use and Distance Education

Even though these basic concepts of copyright still stand, the use of the Internet for delivering instruction both in the classroom and through distance education has changed all the rules involving fair use. It has been suggested that educators routinely violate copyright law when the Internet is used for instruction. Fair use allowances for the classroom change when the Internet is used for distance education, since the Internet is a virtual public display and a distribution of copyrighted material—two of the rights granted to the copyright holder.

Distance education traditionally has described classes that are delivered to a location distant from the originating college or university by any medium. In contrast to classroom instruction that is face-to-face, distance education may involve no face at all, as in the case of a class delivered online with no real-time participation by an instructor. Distance education as it relates to copyright and fair use is instruction that is delivered to a site other than a classroom via any medium. Because of this difference, what is fair use in the classroom may not be fair use in distance education.

For example, an instructor may show legally obtained slides of paintings of the Sistine Chapel in a classroom under the concept of fair use. But if the same class is delivered via the Internet, the slides may not be shown on the class website unless that site is password protected. If access to the website is not limited to members of a class, the showing of the slides on it constitutes public display, which is a right reserved only to the copyright holder.

Public display would also prohibit showing a chart, a picture, or a still from a motion picture over a class website without password protection. In a course that is podcast, it is legal for the instructor to read from literary works but not from dramatic works. All performances of dramatic works are prohibited in distance education without permission. Performances of any work that is neither literary nor, in some cases, musical are excluded from protection under fair use. Hence, all audiovisual works are excluded from fair use in distance education. Audiovisual works include motion pictures, videotapes, and many screen displays from computer programs.

An instructor may, in a distance education class, read from *Moby Dick* but may not show a clip from the motion picture version of that novel. A professor may read an excerpt from a play but may not create a dramatic reading or performance of it.

Clearly this situation and others like it present problems for instruction in the digital age. The Conference on Fair Use attempted to resolve some of these matters, while the Digital Millennium Copyright Act further restricted the fair use of education material delivered via the Internet.

The Conference on Fair Use

In attempting to deal with issues regarding technology and education, a group of librarians, publishers, educators, technical experts, and others met in 1994. This group, the Conference on Fair Use, generated a set of fair use guidelines for various electronic formats in an attempt to meet the problems encountered with education and copyright regarding the Internet. CONFU issued a draft document with proposed guidelines in 1997. The guidelines met with a mixed response.

The CONFU guidelines are not law. What these guidelines represent is an agreement among the organizations that have created them and endorsed them. After three years of discussion, the CONFU group could not reach an agreement over the proposed complicated guidelines, so some organizations support the guidelines and some do not. The major problem with the guidelines is that answers for each issue could not satisfy the diverse needs and concerns of the various groups that convened to draft them.

So what good are the guidelines? Since copyright law is not always clear, librarians must proceed using their best judgment as to what the law allows. If a librarian has inadvertently violated copyright in some manner but has acted using the best guidelines possible, it is very likely that no court would punish the offender.

However, some organizations have approved the guidelines. In no way should these guidelines be considered a safe harbor for those weighing the issues of fair use for digital works. But they can serve as a purposeful attempt to apply fair use and to seek a minimal safe harbor to a given situation involving digital works when a definitive answer is not available. Be warned that the information below is only a summary of the more significant CONFU guidelines.

For distance education, in situations where information is transmitted over the Internet to enrolled students, there have to be "technological limitations" on the students' ability to access the information. This means that only enrolled students can access the information by using a password or a PIN number. For example, access to items placed on electronic reserve has to be restricted by password to only those enrolled in a given class.

Educators may make available to students via the Internet a presentation that they have given to peers such as a workshop or conference presentation.

Educators may retain others' copyrighted multimedia projects in their personal portfolios for later personal uses such as a tenure review.

Educators may use their educational multimedia projects for a period of up to two years after the first use with a class. Use beyond that time period, even for educational purposes, requires permission for each copyrighted portion incorporated in the production.

Up to 10 percent or three minutes, whichever is less, of a copyrighted motion media work may be reproduced or otherwise incorporated as part of a multimedia project for educational purposes.

Up to 10 percent or 1,000 words, whichever is less, of a copyrighted work consisting of text material may be reproduced or otherwise incorporated as part of a multimedia project. An entire poem of less than 250 words may be used, but no more than three poems by one poet, or five poems by different poets from a single anthology, may be used.

Up to 10 percent, but in no event more than thirty seconds, of the music and lyrics from an individual musical work may be reproduced or otherwise incorporated as part of a multimedia project.

A photograph or illustration may be used in its entirety, but no more than five images by an artist or photographer may be reproduced or used as part of an educational multimedia project. When using photographs and illustrations from a published collective work, not more than 10 percent or fifteen images, whichever is less, may be reproduced.

Up to 10 percent or 2,500 fields or cell entries, whichever is less, from a copyrighted database or data table may be reproduced. A "field or cell entry" is either a name, a Social Security number, or the intersection where a row and a column meet on a spreadsheet.

There may be no more than two copies of an educator's educational multimedia project, only one of which may be placed on reserve in a library. An additional copy may be made for preservation purposes but may only be used or copied to replace a use copy that has been lost, stolen, or damaged.

Educators must credit the sources used in all multimedia projects used for educational purposes.

As stated previously, these guidelines are not law. Librarians and educators can use them as a reasonable guide in deciding instances of fair use for educational and library purposes when using electronic media. However, the best guide is still to apply the guidelines for fair use.

The Digital Millennium Copyright Act

The DMCA is not a new copyright law but rather an addendum to the Copyright Revision Act of 1976 that attempts to address some of the issues of copyright in the digital age. There are important items in this law that have a great impact on librarians. The DMCA makes it a crime to circumvent antitheft devices built into software to protect it from piracy. For example, if a faculty member has placed items on electronic reserve for a given class and protected these items with a password that is known only to members of her class, it is illegal for a librarian to try and circumvent that password so that the items placed on reserve can be used by others. If an instructor has purchased software that has protections built into it to prohibit downloading of the text or images on the software, it would be illegal for the instructor to devise a means or to write additional software that would allow others to download images from the protected software.

Along these same lines, the sale or manufacture of devices used to copy protected software is illegal. It is legal, however, for a university faculty member to conduct research into how to break copyright protection devices. The DMCA also gives an exemption to nonprofit libraries and educational institutions under certain specific circumstances to circumvent protection devices and software.

The DMCA also limits the liability of Internet service providers when one of the ISP's customers violates copyright law. This particular issue had been the subject of significant court cases. At the heart of this concept is the liability of the ISP if it did not have knowledge of the illegal activity. AOL, Yahoo!, and other ISPs are well known, but the ISP may even be a library if the library is acting as a gateway to Internet services. In some previous court cases, providing the means to perform illegal activity under copyright law constituted what was called "contributory infringement." But under the DMCA, even if the ISP's service made available the technology to pirate copyrighted works that appeared on the Internet, the ISP is not liable if it had no knowledge of the illegal activity under certain circumstances.

In order to be an ISP, the service provider must register with the Copyright Office. This action requires the identification of a designated "agent." The purpose of the agent is to act as a contact in cases of infringement. Virtually all colleges and universities that maintain a network for the scholarly and informational needs of their academic community would be considered ISPs. It would follow that in order to be protected from liability with regard to the DMCA, all colleges and universities and large school systems would have to identify an "agent." In this way, a small operation may not designate itself as an ISP in an attempt to hide behind the DMCA in protecting itself from liability.

In addition, the DMCA spells out four ways in which the ISP is involved or not involved with infringing material. There is no liability for an ISP if it is involved with simple transitory communications, that is, if the ISP is acting as just a conduit for information and is not providing content itself. An ISP is not liable in cases of system caching, in which the ISP temporarily saves information for easy access; that is, it allows the subscriber to repeatedly get information without contacting the original source. An ISP is not liable if it acts as a web page host and agrees to post notices of take down (see below). And finally, an ISP is not liable under the DMCA if it provides location tools such as links to other sites, as long as it agrees to abide by take down procedures. The point is that although it seems as if the DMCA is protecting ISPs against any liability in cases of infringement, the instances in which protection occurs are quite specific.

A disturbing feature of the DMCA involves what is called "notice and take down provisions." The best way to explain this feature of the DMCA is with an example. Mr. Smith notices that his copyrighted photograph of a dog appears on the website of a company that sells dog toys, DogEToys. Smith has not licensed or permitted DogEToys to use his photograph. Smith sends a written notification to USOnline, the ISP on which the offending photograph appears, stating that the photograph appears without his permission. According to the DMCA, USOnline is required to "expeditiously" remove or block access to the offending page. By doing this, USOnline is exempt from any liability from the copyright holder, Smith, or from the web page owner, DogEToys.

Once the offending material has been removed by USOnline, that company has to take additional steps to protect the rights of DogEToys. In what are termed "notice and put back procedures," USOnline must take "reasonable steps" to notify DogEToys that the web page has been removed from USOnline's servers. DogEToys then must send a counternotice to USOnline stating that the material in question was legal or was misidentified as non-licensed information, or else it must accept the removal of the offending material.

To remain exempt from liability, USOnline must then provide a copy of this statement to Mr. Smith. After receiving this statement, Smith must notify USOnline that a court action has been initiated, or else USOnline has to restore the offending material. After receiving the first counternotice from DogEToys and receiving no notice from Smith that a court action is imminent, USOnline must put back the offending material in no less than ten days but not more than fourteen days to escape liability.

The disturbing part, other than their complicated procedures, of these "notice and take down provisions" is that material can be removed from the Internet for ten to fourteen days simply by the accusation of a copyright holder who may or may not have any evidence that a case of copyright infringement has been demonstrated. In situations like the example above where a commercial website selling goods on its site is shut down, the monetary damage could be significant; however, the ISP is immune from liability if it follows the procedures set forth in the DMCA.

In no other area of law may a person or company's source of income be cut off simply on the basis of an accusation of one party and be left with restrictions on the possibility of suit of one of the offending parties. Normally, in U.S. law, evidence must be produced before any action is taken to limit the First Amendment rights of any party.

In summary, the issues of copyright and the Internet are not ephemeral things. The problems of new technology have always been a part of copyright law and interpretation. The issues with Napster or YouTube services allowing easy copying of protected property will occur repeatedly as changes in technology make obsolete the safeguards placed on them previously. Groups representing copyright holders, industry, artists, librarians, and educators will continue to prepare and try out guidelines for the safe use and handling of intellectual property in the digital age.

Intellectual Property Court Cases

Over the last 200 years, legal cases have helped to decide the complicated issues of interpreting copyright protection. Many of these cases have been significant in that the decision reached determined the application of copyright law from that point on. This section describes some of these cases and the points of law that made each one significant in the application of copyright in the United States.

There have as yet been no court cases that test the legality of certain aspects of copyright as it applies to the Internet. For example, the public "broadcast" of a play over the Internet by a teacher without limiting access to members of a class has not been challenged. The DMCA has tried to address some of the concerns that arise from electronic media. In pre-DMCA court cases where electronic media have been an issue in copyright disputes, the courts have applied the traditional principles of copyright law to the new technologies in predictable ways. For example, the fact that a work appears on a website does not give license to a viewer of that work to copy it. Courts have not hesitated to rule that copying a work in a computer's random access memory (RAM), even if a temporary copy, is more than transitory use and constitutes a reproduction subject to control of the copyright holder (*MAI Systems Corp. v. Peak Computer, Inc.*, 991 F.2d 511, 519). The uploading and downloading of copyrighted works outside the framework of fair use have consistently been found to be infringements (*Playboy Enterprises v. Frena*, 839 F.Supp. 1552).

The responsibilities of Internet service providers have been explored in several cases. In 1994 the first case involving an ISP, *MAI v. Peak,* established the definition of "copy" as it applies to electronic media. In this landmark decision, it was determined by the court that the simple act of loading software into a computer's RAM is considered making a copy under the copyright law. In a related case, *Marobie-FL v. NAFED,* it was further determined that the length of time copies remain in RAM is irrelevant. There is no safe time to perform a copying procedure before it is deemed infringement.

Other cases have implied liability for ISPs and bulletin board service (BBS) operators. In *Playboy Enterprises v. Frena* (1993 and pre-DMCA), a BBS that contained copyrighted pictures owned by Playboy was found liable even though the BBS operator did not make the copies himself and was proven not to have known about the existence of them on his BBS, since the servers work automatically. In effect the BBS operator was liable for merely providing a means by which to make copies. If this logic were extended, ISPs could be held liable for the activities of their users. However, this case was ruled on before the DMCA attempted to sort out the responsibilities of ISPs in copyright matters.

The copyright responsibilities of ISPs for the activities of others were further explored in a 1995 case, *Religious Technology Center v. Netcom* (907 F.Supp. 1361; 1995 U.S. Dist. LEXIS 18173). Files containing copyrighted materials owned by the Church of Scientology were placed on an Internet newsgroup through a server controlled by Netcom. The user who placed the files actually used a local bulletin board system that provided Internet access through Netcom. The church wanted the material removed from Netcom servers. When Netcom refused to remove the materials, the church went to court.

The court found that neither Netcom nor the BBS had directly infringed on copyright, since neither party took any action to cause copies to be made. There was no monetary award made to the church; however, the court found that Netcom might be liable for contributory infringement by materially contributing to infringement by the Internet user. The court stated that if Netcom knew about the copyrighted materials on its server, it should have removed them. But before a decision was made in this case, the parties settled out of court. It is also significant that this case took place in 1995, before the DMCA.

Cases decided since Netcom have followed the same analysis. A BBS operator who knowingly allowed users to upload and download copyrighted SEGA video games was determined not to be a direct infringer, but since the operator knew about the activity, he was guilty under the theory of contributory infringement.

In 1996 a case between the Long Island newspaper *Newsday* and a photography agency was one of the first to involve what is termed "digital plagiarism" of an image nearly too small to see. The case involved a photomontage, a large photograph made of thousands of tiny photographs. In the case, a *Newsday* illustrator had copied, without permission, a photo by James Porto as part of a larger computer-generated photomontage for its cover page. The photo agency was awarded damages by the court.

Also in 1996, Adobe Photoshop's Image Club marketed a CD with images of paintings by Edward Hopper and Georgia O'Keefe, among others. The image of Hopper's painting *Lighthouse* is owned by the Dallas Museum of Art, and O'Keefe's images are owned by the O'Keefe Foundation. Adobe secured the images from a company called Planet Art. Adobe was assured by Planet Art that the images were royalty-free, even though the Hopper *Lighthouse* carried a copyright symbol. As the situation progressed, it was learned that Planet Art had simply scanned the images from an art catalog. Neither the Dallas Museum nor the O'Keefe Foundation was able to locate anyone associated with Planet Art. On receiving cease and desist letters from the Dallas Museum, Adobe was forced to destroy 350 unsold CDs and had to inform previous buyers of the CD that the images on it were copyrighted and could not be used without permission.

In this particular case the doctrine of "first sale" comes into play. In the copyright law (Copyright Revision Act of 1976, 109a), first sale is a concept that allows the owner of a lawfully obtained work to give or sell that copy to another without permission, but it does not allow the obtained work to be copied. For example, if a person buys a book, he or she may give *that* book to another person but cannot make a copy of that book. If a person buys a painting, he or she may give or sell that painting to another but may not make copies of the painting. Even though a painting is purchased, the copyright remains with the artist. Although the Dallas Museum of Art owned the rights to Hopper's *Lighthouse,* this is not always the case with works owned by museums. According to first sale doctrine, even though a museum may purchase a piece of art, it does not also purchase the right to reproduce or copy that piece of art unless the artist specifically grants that right to the purchaser. The sticking point here is that there is no clear agreement as to whether a display of a work on a remote computer is a permitted copy or a new copy being generated. While copyright law permits a user to give another user a physical copy of a legally obtained book, the law prohibits a user from transmitting a digital copy of that same book without permission.

The courts have thus decided on a few landmark cases that begin to sort out the problems of copyright as it applies to electronic media. Many other aspects of copyright protection, such as whether or not audiovisual material on a website constitutes a "broadcast," have not been decided. In the cases decided so far, the courts have tended to treat electronic media as they would other media and have decided in favor of the copyright owner. This trend disturbs some, since judgments consistently in favor of the copyright holders limit the fair use of electronic material for educational purposes. Although the DMCA has attempted to resolve some of these issues, this law seems to be driven by the publishing industry and the entertainment industry, which are seeking to protect their financial stake in the Internet at the risk of stifling the legitimate access to information and the needs of education.

There are those who believe that the copyright law does apply to the new digital media, just as when new technologies such as film and television came along, the existing copyright law was shown to be applicable to them. But since Congress has seen fit to pass the DMCA, it is obvious that the new digital media do have some unique features that need to be addressed in future court cases.

Internationally the problems of copyright are magnified. In the United States there are laws and procedures for protecting copyright that are commonly recognized. In other countries, the effort to protect one's copyright does not always have a clearly defined path. It has been estimated that 60 percent of all copyrighted materials sold in Russia—including movies, music, software, and books—are pirated. Much of this activity is made possible by peer-to-peer (P2P) services such as Kazaa.

P2P services operate by referring to the benchmark case of *Sony v. Universal City Studios.* This case decided that technology that is capable of performing illegal activities—in this case the ability of the videocassette recorder to copy protected films—is not thereby illegal, since the technology may also duplicate legally obtained videotapes; the technology is legal as long as it is capable of substantial non-infringing uses. P2P services maintain that although some may use their services to copy or distribute protected works, the P2P services may also be used for legal activities.

In 2005 the Supreme Court unanimously decided an important case known as *MGM v. Grokster.* Twenty-eight of the world's largest entertainment companies brought a lawsuit against the makers of the Morpheus, Grokster, and Kazaa software products, aiming to set a precedent to use against other technology companies (P2P and otherwise). This case raised a fundamental question between copyright and innovation: when should the distributor of a multipurpose tool be held liable for the infringements that may be committed by end users of that tool? MGM alleged vicarious and contributory copyright infringement by Grokster for distributing peer-to-peer file-sharing software. According to MGM, over 90 percent of the material exchanged using Grokster's file-sharing software is copyrighted material, and therefore copyright infringement occurs every time users exchange the information. MGM contended that Grokster contributes to this infringement by making the file-sharing software available to the public.

The Ninth Circuit Court held that Grokster was not liable for contributory infringement because it lacked sufficient knowledge of the copyright infringement and it did not materially contribute to the infringement. According to the court, the peer-to-peer file-sharing software distributed by Grokster was capable of substantial non-infringing uses. But the case eventually worked its way up to the U.S. Supreme Court, which overturned the circuit court's decision primarily on the concept of "substantial" non-infringing uses that were defined in the *Sony v. Universal City Studios* decision. Since it was shown that 90 percent of Grokster's activity involved illegal use, its use as a legal file-sharing business was minimal.

Google, which seems to be the leader in recent intellectual property disputes, recently announced its $1.65 billion purchase of YouTube, an Internet site that shares video clips sent in by Internet users. YouTube delivers 100 million clips a day to anybody wishing to view them—or download them. Many users lift segments of TV programs and movies without seeking permission by the copyright holders. When YouTube was a small Internet company, intellectual property lawyers didn't go after its profits from copyright violations, but now that YouTube is part of a $9.6 billion company, the tide may change. In anticipation of this, YouTube began removing all clips from the Comedy Central TV network, including those from *The Daily Show* and *The Colbert Report,* which are some of the most widely viewed clips on YouTube. In the first week of this process, YouTube removed 30,000 clips.

Another Google venture, the Google Book Project, has drawn a lot of attention from publishers. The Book Project wants to digitize all of a library's holdings and, initially, make the content searchable like a giant index. The Authors Guild and a group of major publishing houses have filed suits charging Google with copyright infringement on a massive scale. Google argues that under the fair use provisions of copyright law, it has a perfect right to let its users search the text of copyrighted works—as long as, once the search is complete, it only shows them what it calls "snippets" of those works. The authors and publishers say that in order to find and display those snippets, Google must first copy whole books without permission. Google announced the library scanning project in December 2004 and currently has four library partners: Stanford University, Oxford University, the University of Michigan, and the New York Public Library.

Google maintains that its use of copyrighted works is "transformative," part of the legal definition of fair use, and that a simple search doesn't hurt the marketplace for a book—another fair use criterion. All those involved in IP issues are waiting for suits involving the Google Book Project to work their way through the courts.

In yet another IP dispute involving Google, Perfect 10, an entertainment publisher, sued Google and Amazon.com for copyright infringement. Perfect 10 asked the court to order Google and Amazon.com to stop displaying thumbnail images of Perfect 10 female models in their image search results and to also stop users from linking directly to third-party sites that host and serve infringing full-size images of the models.

The initial question was whether Google's use of Perfect 10's images was an infringing use. The district court hearing the case began by applying what it referred to as the "server test." Under the server test, a search engine, such as Google, is capable of copyright infringement only if it actually stores the copyrighted images on its own servers. The court determined that Google creates and stores thumbnails of Perfect 10's copyrighted images on its servers, thus making it liable for copyright infringement. However, the court basically provided Google with a "safe harbor" with respect to the full-size images. Again applying the server test, the court determined that Google would likely not be found liable for infringement of the full-size images that are displayed not from Google's own servers but via direct linking to third-party websites, that is, third-party servers. Google merely provides the link, not the content, and as such, Perfect 10's claim of direct infringement with respect to these actions would likely fail.

The court's decision in *Perfect 10 v. Google* has far-reaching implications for other companies engaged in the business of facilitating and improving access to information on the Internet. Given the flexibility of the fair use doctrine and the pace at which evolving technologies are reaching the marketplace, there may be other applications that have to date qualified as fair use but that now may no longer benefit from such protection. Companies may find new commercial applications for their copyrighted materials, and other courts may see fit to apply this analysis to such applications, thus potentially narrowing the fair use doctrine as it could be applied to the reproduction of copyrighted works over the Internet and other technologies.

Certainly, the court's decision seems to be directed at those instances where the copyrighted work, in its thumbnail-sized incarnation, is offered for sale for download to a mobile phone or other device. But in so holding, the court has rejected the fair use defense for those works that, while offered for sale, will never be purchased for download. Thus, where use of a thumbnail was protected under fair use principles one day, such use would seem to have lost that status the next with no apparent gain to the copyright holder and with a net loss to the researching public. This seems a paradoxical result. Moreover, there is the practical issue of how a search engine, before displaying an image, will know whether the thumbnail version of that work is available for purchase from the copyright holder. It appears, given the preliminary nature of the decision, and upon further appeal or review of a full evidentiary record at the conclusion of the litigation, that a reevaluation of the fair use defense might be in order.

Questions and Answers about Copyright

Q   What does copyright protect?

A   Copyright, a form of intellectual property law, protects original works of authorship, including literary, dramatic, musical, and artistic works such as poetry, novels, movies, songs, computer software, and architecture.

Q   What does copyright not protect?

A   It does not protect facts, ideas, systems, methods of operation, slogans or sayings, government documents, recipes, and lists of ingredients, although it may protect the way these things are expressed.

Q   If a work does not have a copyright symbol or notice, is it a protected work?

A   A copyright symbol or worded notice has not been required by law since 1988.

Q   Since virtually everything on the Internet is easily downloaded and copied, is everything on the Internet in the public domain?

A   Virtually everything on the Internet is copyrighted and cannot be copied freely without permission. Being able to copy freely does not constitute legality.

Q   Is contacting a copyright holder for permission to use copyrighted material always a good idea?

A   No. The purpose of fair use is to allow copying under certain conditions without permission. One should attempt to contact a copyright holder only after fair use has been ruled out.

Q   May students use pages from government documents without permission for reports and papers?

A   Yes. Anybody may use government documents for whatever purpose without permission. Government documents are not copyrighted.

Q   Does one have to register a work with the Copyright Office in order to claim copyright?

A   No. Copyright is assumed on creation of the work. Registering the work gives one a better legal framework from which to defend a work against infringers, but it is not necessary.

Q   If a person writes original stories based on characters in another author's book, does the new work belong exclusively to its own author?

A   One of the rights that belongs to a copyright holder is the right to prepare derivative works. Basing a story on characters that appear in another author's copyrighted book is a violation of copyright.

Q   A school transcribes the lyrics from the album *Grease* and performs it as the school mini-musical. A student plays the music by ear on the piano, no sheet music is purchased or used, and the students perform every song. There is no admission charge. Is this a violation of copyright?

A   Yes. Copyright holders sell the performance rights to schools in a very specific way. It doesn't matter that there was no sheet music used, or that no admission was charged, or that this is an educational use. The school has to buy the performance rights.

Q   The TV show *I Love Lucy* has an episode on personal hygiene that a health teacher tapes to use the following week in class. The teacher asks the local TV station that broadcast the program for copyright permission. Can the station deny this permission?

A   No. It doesn't hold the copyright on *I Love Lucy.* However, it is not legal for the school to show this taped program. A public display of the entire program is a violation of copyright without obtaining permission.

Q   When is my work protected?

A   Your work is under copyright protection the moment it is created and fixed in a tangible form so that it is perceptible either directly or with the aid of a machine or device.

Q   How can I obtain copies of someone else's work and/or registration certificate?

A   The Copyright Office will not honor a request for a copy of someone else's work without written authorization from the owner or from his or her designated agent if that work is still under copyright protection, unless the work is involved in litigation. Written permission from the copyright owner or a litigation statement is required before copies can be made available. A certificate of registration for any registered work can be obtained for a fee of $25.

Q   Why should I register my work if copyright protection is automatic?

A   Registration is recommended for a number of reasons. Many choose to register their works because they wish to have the facts of their copyright on the public record and have a certificate of registration. Registered works may be eligible for statutory damages and attorney's fees in successful litigation. Finally, if registration occurs within five years of publication, it is considered prima facie evidence in a court of law.

Q   Is the Copyright Office the only place to register a copyright?

A   Although copyright application forms may be available in public libraries and some reference books, the U.S. Copyright Office is the only office that can accept applications and issue registrations.

Q How do I register my copyright?

A To register a work, you need to submit a completed application form, a nonrefundable filing fee, and a nonreturnable copy or copies of the work to be registered.

Q How long does the registration process take?

A The time the Copyright Office requires to process an application varies, depending on the amount of material the office is receiving. You may generally expect a certificate of registration within eight months of submission.

Q What is the registration fee?

A The current filing fee is $45 per application. Generally, each work requires a separate application.

Q Can I use copies of the application form to register my copyright?

A Yes, you can make copies of application forms if they meet the following criteria: they must be photocopied back-to-back and head-to-head on a single sheet of 8½-by-11-inch white paper. In other words, your copy must look just like the original.

Q What is a deposit?

A A deposit is usually one copy (if unpublished) or two copies (if published) of the work to be registered for copyright. In certain cases, such as works of visual art, identifying material such as a photograph may be used instead. The deposit is sent with the application and fee and becomes the property of the Copyright Office.

Q Do I have to send in my work? Do I get it back?

A Yes, you must send the required copy or copies of the work to be registered. These copies will not be returned. Upon their deposit in the Copyright Office, under sections 407 and 408 of the copyright law, all copies, audio recordings, and identifying material, including those deposited in connection with claims that have been refused registration, are the property of the U.S. government.

Q May I register more than one work on the same application? Where do I list the titles?

A You may register unpublished works as a collection on one application with one title for the entire collection if certain conditions are met. It is not necessary to list the individual titles in your collection, although you may do so by completing a "continuation sheet." Published works may only be registered as a collection if they were actually first published as a collection and if other requirements have been met.

Q What is the difference between the Copyright Office's form PA and form SR?

A These forms are for registering two different types of copyrightable subject matter that may be embodied in a recording. Form PA is used for the registration of music and lyrics (as well as other works of the performing arts), even if your song is on a cassette. Form SR is used for registering the performance and production of a particular recording of sounds.

Q   Do I have to renew my copyright?

A   No. Works created on or after January 1, 1978, are not subject to renewal registration. As to works published or registered prior to January 1, 1978, renewal registration is optional after twenty-eight years but does provide certain legal advantages.

Q   Can I submit my manuscript on a computer disk?

A   No. There are many different software formats, and the Copyright Office does not have the equipment to accommodate all of them. Therefore, the Copyright Office still generally requires a printed copy or audio recording of the work for deposit.

Q   How do I protect my recipe?

A   A mere listing of ingredients is not protected under copyright law. However, where a recipe or formula is accompanied by substantial literary expression in the form of an explanation or directions, or when there is a collection of recipes as in a cookbook, there may be a basis for copyright protection.

Q   Can copyrighted materials used in multimedia projects remain in a student's portfolio forever?

A   Yes. As long as the material is not publicly distributed, the student may archive her work.

Q   Does copyright now protect architecture?

A   Yes. Architectural works became subject to copyright protection on December 1, 1990. The copyright law defines an "architectural work" as "the design of a building embodied in any tangible medium of expression, including a building, architectural plans, or drawings." Copyright protection extends to any architectural work created on or after December 1, 1990, and any architectural work that on or after December 1, 1990, was not constructed but was embodied in unpublished plans or drawings. Architectural works embodied in buildings constructed prior to December 1, 1990, are not eligible for copyright protection.

Q   Can I register a diary I found in my grandmother's attic?

A   You can register copyright in the diary only if you are the transferee (by will or by inheritance). Copyright is the right of the author of the work or the author's heirs or assignees, not of the one who only owns or possesses the physical work itself.

Q   Can foreigners register their works in the United States?

A   Any work that is protected by U.S. copyright law can be registered. This includes many works of foreign origin. All works that are unpublished, regardless of the nationality of the author, are protected in the United States. Works that are first published in the United States or in a country with which we have a copyright treaty or that are created by a citizen or legal resident of a country with which we have a copyright treaty are also protected and may therefore be registered with the U.S. Copyright Office.

Q What is an author?

A Under the copyright law, the creator of the original expression in a work is its author. The author is also the owner of copyright unless there is a written agreement by which the author assigns the copyright to another person or entity, such as a publisher. In cases of works made for hire, the employer or commissioning party is considered to be the author.

Q What is a work made for hire?

A Although the general rule is that the person who creates a work is its author, there is an exception to this principle. A work made for hire is a work prepared by an employee within the scope of his or her employment, or a work specially ordered or commissioned in certain specified circumstances. When a work qualifies as a work made for hire, the employer or commissioning party is considered to be the author.

Q Can a minor claim copyright?

A Minors may claim copyright, and the Copyright Office does issue registrations to minors, but state laws may regulate the business dealings involving copyrights owned by minors. For information on relevant state laws, consult an attorney.

Q Do I have to use my real name on the application form? Can I use a stage name or a pen name?

A There is no legal requirement that the author be identified by his or her real name on the application form.

Q What is publication?

A The word *publication* has a technical meaning in copyright law. According to the statute, "publication is the distribution of copies or phono records of a work to the public by sale or other transfer of ownership, or by rental, lease, or lending. The offering to distribute copies or phono records to a group of persons for purposes of further distribution, public performance, or public display constitutes publication. A public performance or display of a work does not of itself constitute publication." Generally, publication occurs on the date on which copies of the work are first made available to the public.

Q Does my work have to be published to be protected?

A Publication is not necessary for copyright protection.

Q Are copyrights transferable?

A Yes. Like any other property, the owner may transfer all or part of the rights in a work to another.

Q Can I copyright the name of my band?

A No. Copyright law does not protect names. Some names may be protected under trademark law, however.

Q   How do I copyright a name, title, slogan, or logo?

A   Copyright does not protect names, titles, slogans, or short phrases. In some cases, these things may be protected as trademarks. However, copyright protection may be available for logo artwork that contains sufficient authorship. In some circumstances, an artistic logo may also be protected as a trademark.

Q   How do I protect my idea?

A   Copyright does not protect ideas, concepts, systems, or methods of doing something. You may express your ideas in writing or drawings and claim copyright in your description, but be aware that copyright will not protect the idea itself as revealed in your written or artistic work.

Q   How long does copyright last?

A   The Sonny Bono Copyright Term Extension Act, signed into law on October 27, 1998, amended the provisions concerning the duration of copyright protection. Under the act, the terms of copyright were generally extended for an additional 20 years. Specific provisions are as follows:

  • For works created after January 1, 1978, copyright protection will endure for the life of the author plus an additional 70 years. In the case of a joint work, the term lasts for 70 years after the last surviving author's death. For anonymous and pseudonymous works and works made for hire, the term is 95 years from the year of first publication or 120 years from the year of creation, whichever expires first.

  • For works created but not published or registered before January 1, 1978, the term endures for the life of the author plus 70 years but in no case will expire earlier than December 31, 2002. If the work was published before December 31, 2002, the term will not expire before December 31, 2047.

  • For pre-1978 works still in their original or renewal term of copyright, the total term is extended to 95 years from the date that copyright was originally secured.

Q   How much do I have to change in my own work to make a new claim of copyright?

A   You may make a new claim in your work if the changes are substantial and creative—something more than just editorial changes or minor changes. This would qualify as a new derivative work. For instance, simply making spelling corrections throughout a work does not warrant a new registration—but adding an additional chapter would.

Q   How do I get my work into the Library of Congress?

A   Copies of works deposited for copyright registration or in fulfillment of the mandatory deposit requirement are available to the Library of Congress for its collections. The library reserves the right to select or reject any published work for its permanent collections based on the research needs of Congress, the nation's scholars, and of the nation's libraries.

Q   What is a copyright notice? How do I put a copyright notice on my work?

A   A copyright notice is an identifier placed on copies of the work to inform the world of copyright ownership. While use of a copyright notice was once required as a condition of copyright protection, it is now optional. Use of the notice is the responsibility of the copyright owner and does not require advance permission from, or registration with, the Copyright Office.

Q   How do I collect royalties?

A   The collection of royalties is usually a matter of private arrangement between an author and publisher or other users of the author's work. The Copyright Office plays no role in the execution of contractual terms or business practices. There are copyright licensing organizations and publication rights clearinghouses that distribute royalties for their members.

Q   Somebody infringed my copyright. What can I do?

A   A party may seek to protect his or her copyrights against unauthorized use by filing a civil lawsuit in a federal district court. If you believe that your copyright has been infringed, consult an attorney. In cases of willful infringement for profit, the U.S. attorney may initiate a criminal investigation.

Q   Is my copyright good in other countries?

A   The United States has copyright relations with more than 100 countries throughout the world, and as a result of these agreements, we honor each other's citizens' copyrights. However, the United States does not have such copyright relationships with every country.

Q   How do I get permission to use somebody else's work?

A   You can ask for it. If you know who the copyright owner is, you may contact the owner directly. If you are not certain about the ownership or have other related questions, you may wish to request the Copyright Office to conduct a search of its records for a fee of $65 per hour.

Q   Could I be sued for using somebody else's work? How about quotes or samples?

A   If you use a copyrighted work without authorization, the owner may be entitled to bring an infringement action against you. There are circumstances under the fair use doctrine where a quote or a sample may be used without permission. However, in cases of doubt, the Copyright Office recommends that permission be obtained.

Q   Is it permissible to use copyrighted material if there is no charge for the final work the copyrighted material is used in?

A   Not always. One of the four guidelines for fair use is that the copyrighted material used does not detrimentally affect the value of the copyrighted material, but this is not the only guideline. Other factors may make this practice illegal even if is for a nonprofit use.

Q   Is using a short excerpt from a book for scholarly use considered fair use?

A   Not always. A short excerpt from a children's book may actually constitute a significant portion of that book and would not be allowed under fair use guidelines.

The important issue is what part of the entire work the excerpt constitutes, not the size of the excerpt itself.

Q   A teacher taped an *ABC News* report showing Bill Clinton leaving the White House. She made it at home on her VCR. She uses the entire program every year in her classroom. Is this fair use?

A   No. Publicly broadcast news events can only be shown for ten days afterward unless the copyright holder grants greater allowances for educators.

Q   The owner of the local video store donates one videotape rental-free to the school every Friday. The video is shown in a classroom to reward students with perfect attendance. Is this fair use?

A   No. Reward is explicitly excluded under copyright guidelines. To show a movie for entertainment purposes, one must obtain a version from an authorized distributor who can license one to show.

Q   A teacher rents *Gone with the Wind* to show the scene of the burning of Atlanta one time to her class while studying the Civil War. Is this fair use?

A   Yes, this is a clear example of fair use.

Q   A school purchases one copy of a typing tutorial program, which is housed in the library. It is checked out to individual students to take home for a week and load onto their home computers. Each student is required to erase the program at the end of the one week. Is this fair use?

A   Yes. The school must make serious efforts, however, to ensure that the program is erased from the home computers.

Q   A student doing a report discovers how to copy several frames of the Zapruder film of the Kennedy assassination from an online encyclopedia. He presents the report to his classmates and then posts it on the school's network. Is this fair use?

A   Yes, but there are two important items that make this fair use. First, the length of the clip is short, and second, its use is for educational purposes. But it is also important that the school network is not accessible to the outside world.

Q   A student finds a photo online dramatizing a Viking landing in America. Since the school symbol is the Viking, she uses this photo on the school's web page, giving credit to the site from which it was copied. Is this fair use?

A   No. Internet pages are copyrighted automatically. The student cannot post anything for the general public without permission, even if credit is given. Use in a class report would have been fair use.

Q   A student doing a multimedia art project uses copyrighted images of Frank Lloyd Wright buildings downloaded from the Web. She submits this project to a competition for classroom multimedia projects. Is this covered under fair use?

A   Yes, as long as the competition was expressly for classroom work by students. If the resulting projects were distributed or posted at a website, this would not be fair use.

Q An instructional services employee at a high school tapes the *CBS News* every day in case teachers need it. Is this fair use?

A No. Schools may not tape in anticipation of requests. They can act only on actual requests.

Q A high school video class produces a student video that is sold at community events to raise money for video equipment for the school. The students use well-known popular music clips in the video. The money all goes to the school and the songs are fully listed in the credits. Is this fair use?

A No. This is not instructional or educational use. The fact that money is being charged is irrelevant. The infringement lies in the use of copyrighted materials for noninstructional purposes.

Q Are advertising slogans, written statements on T-shirts, or bumper sticker sayings, such as "Just Do It," protected by copyright?

A No. Copyright is reserved for prose, poetry, artistic works, computer programs, movies, and the like. Copyright does not protect slogans or short phrases. In some cases, however, these things may be protected as trademarks; advertising slogans are trademarks.

Q Can copyright be used to protect ideas, systems, or methods of doing things?

A No. Copyright can be issued only on a form of expression, not the idea per se.

Q Before a copyright is issued, does the Copyright Office go through an extensive search, in much the same way that the PTO does for patents and trademarks?

A No. The Copyright Office doesn't care if a work is previously copyrighted or not. If there is an infringement on copyright, it is up to the individual and the courts to straighten things out.

Q Can sounds be copyrighted?

A Yes, although there are very few of them. The MGM lion's roar and the NBC chime are two examples. Recently Harley-Davidson attempted to copyright the sound of its motorcycle engine, claiming the sound was unique and distinctive. As of this writing, the company has not been successful.

Five

Trademarks

A trademark is a word, slogan, design, symbol, or a color, smell, product configuration, or combination of these used to identify the source of origin of particular goods and services and to distinguish these from the goods and services of others. Although some trademarks, such as the Nike "swoosh" or the arches of McDonald's, are easily recognizable, other trademarks, while familiar, are not seen as trademarks. For example, the green color of John Deere farm equipment is a trademark, as are the pink color of Owens-Corning fiberglass and the orange color of disposable medical face masks sold by Kimberly-Clark.

Some of the best trademarks are those that evoke mental images, such as the name Slim-Fast. Made-up words such as Exxon are easy to protect, since the name exists only in its usage for that company's goods and services. Other strong trademarks are names that are unexpected for the good or service they represent, such as Amazon for an online bookstore. And a distinctive graphic design also makes a good trademark, like the Playboy bunny recognized the world over.

Internet domain names are trademarks. The importance of having a well-known domain name such as yahoo.com or a domain name that is descriptive of an entire discipline, for example, business.com, can mean big profits for the individual or company that owns the right domain name. For example, the domain name sex .com was sold in 2006 for $12 million. In the digital age, cybersquatting has become a problem related to trademarks used as domain names. Cybersquatting is the practice of registering a domain name that has the name of a well-known company or business (or its products) and then selling that domain name to the company for a profit, sometimes an exorbitant one.

The Google trademark is so popular that the word *google* became a verb in *Merriam-Webster's Collegiate Dictionary* in 2006. This created a dilemma for Google, since the generic use of a trademark can lead to loss of its protection, as has happened to trademarks such as Kleenex, which is used generically to refer to paper tissues. Google is currently vigorously discouraging generic usage of its domain name.

Some things cannot be registered as trademarks. Marks that are purely descriptive or are based upon a person's name or geographic location are unprotectable unless the mark develops a secondary meaning that relates directly to a good or service. Examples of this would be Ben & Jerry's, New York Life, and Jiffy Lube. Slogans such as Nike's "Just Do It" can be trademarked but not copyrighted.

Other things that cannot be trademarked are marks that are similar to existing marks. One recent suit by Cisco Systems alleges that Apple's iPhone name is owned by Cisco and cannot be used by Apple. However, Apple maintains that the use is permitted since the products in question, Cisco's cell phone and Apple's phone/Internet device/e-mail device/MP3 player, are materially different. Apple won a trademark suit in 2006 against Apple Corps, the Beatles' recording company, over use of an apple logo. The Apple Computer apple has a bite taken out of it, while the Apple Corps apple is a shiny green apple. Although both logos are used to represent companies in the music business, the courts ruled that the two logos are different enough to not cause confusion in the mind of the public.

Generic terms, such as a soft drink called Soda, and the titles of books or movies unless used to mark a series of goods or services, such as Star Wars Action Figures, cannot be trademarked. Marks considered immoral, scandalous, or deceptive also cannot be trademarked, likewise marks that disparage persons, institutions, or beliefs. Trademarks incorporating flags or coats of arms are not permitted, and names or images of a living person are not permitted without his or her permission. The name of a living president cannot be trademarked, and the name of a dead president cannot be trademarked if the president's wife is still living!

Benefits of Registering a Trademark

The registration of a mark as a trademark is not required, but the benefits of registering far outweigh the time and expense of registration. The primary advantage of registration is that a registered federal trademark shows documented ownership of the mark: ownership that determines and verifies, through a fairly rigorous application process, that the registered mark is unique. The act of registering the mark and having the mark published in the *Official Gazette* of the Patent and Trademark Office gives nationwide notice of the trademark owner and entitles only the registered owner to use the mark nationwide.

There are two types of registration, state and federal. By federally registering a mark, broader rights are conveyed to the owner than those of a state trademark. Federal registration also eliminates the tedious process of registering the mark in each of the states in which the owner does business.

Registration establishes the first date of usage, which can be a valuable point in cases of infringement. It gives greater rights than does a common law trademark in that it prevents others from claiming rights to your mark if it is only used and not registered. By registering and publishing a mark, the owner makes it readily discoverable through a trademark search by others and provides a notice to those considering using a similar mark.

The registration itself is prima facie evidence of ownership, validity, and its owner's exclusive rights. The registration is conclusive evidence and should eliminate all subsequent attempts by others to use the mark without permission. In addition, court actions involving trademark disputes are *federal* court cases and provide for damages and costs possibly triple those of actions in other courts. Infringement on a federally registered trademark also carries criminal penalties for counterfeiting or infringing on the mark. Having a federal trademark means that the owner can stop the importation of goods that bear an infringing mark. And finally, federally registering a trademark means that the owner has the right to use the ® symbol.

A word here about trademark symbols is helpful. There are five symbols or phrases to identify trademarked goods or services: ®, ™, SM, "Registered in the U.S. Patent and Trademark Office," and "Reg. U.S. Pat. & Tm. Off." The ® symbol is used to identify a trademark that is federally registered. A user of this symbol cannot use it until the mark is registered. It is unlawful to use ® for unregistered goods and services or even if the mark is pending registration; however, a mark owner is not required by law to use an identifying symbol.

The ™ symbol is used to notify the public of rights claimed on a mark. The symbol denotes that the mark is not federally registered and may or may not be valid. Usually mark owners will use ™ before registration is granted. The SM symbol means the same thing as ™ except that it is used on services rather than on goods.

Considering the rights given by registering a mark, the process for application is relatively easy. However, in some cases, a trademark examiner for any number of reasons refuses registration of a mark. For example, as stated earlier, if the mark being registered is merely ornamental and is not a mark that uniquely identifies goods or services, it cannot be registered. If the mark is simply the surname of the applicant, it can be refused. Obviously, marks that resemble existing registered trademarks, or that could cause confusion in the mind of the consumer because they are similar to other trademarks or marks, or that are deliberately deceptive in this regard, are refused registration. Marks that are simply descriptive of the product are not permitted. In one case a patented item called an "Electric Fork" was denied trademark registration because it simply described the item.

The owner of a federal registration is presumed to be the owner of the trademark for the goods and services specified in the registration and to be entitled to use the mark nationwide. The owner of a trademark that is not registered is not automatically presumed to be its *owner* but merely the party that is using the mark. A consumer can readily see the difference. A registered trademark carries the symbol ®; a nonregistered mark uses the symbol ™.

Federal protection is national, whereas state protection is limited to the state where the mark has been used. A prior federal registration of a mark preempts subsequent state trademark rights, but prior state use or registration is not pre-empted by subsequent federal registration.

For example, if a car wash in the state of Ohio registers the trademark White Glove Car Care in that state, that mark is protected against a subsequent national franchise with an *unregistered* trademark called White Glove Car Care coming into the state and doing business there under the same name. The company owning the unregistered trademark, White Glove Car Care, may have been unaware that there was a state trademark of the same name, since no search was performed of existing state and federal marks; the company just chose that name. Rather than changing the name of a national franchise, in this situation, there is usually a monetary settlement to the state trademark owner to change the name of its business. However, the state trademark owner cannot be forced to change the business name simply because an unregistered national trademark is doing business in a given state. A registered federal trademark on White Glove Car Care is unlikely, since a search of trademarks would have discovered this registered state trademark and would have prohibited registering the mark White Glove Car Care federally.

There are two related but distinct types of rights in a trademark: the right to register and the right to use. Generally, the first party who either uses a mark in commerce or files an application in the PTO has the ultimate right to register that mark. The right to use a mark can be more complicated to determine. This is particularly true when two parties have begun use of the same or similar marks without knowledge of one another and neither has a federal registration. Only a court can render a decision about the right to use the mark. This is why it is vitally important to federally register a trademark rather than simply use the trademark in commerce without registration.

Unlike copyrights or patents, trademark rights can last indefinitely if the owner continues to use the mark to identify its goods or services. The term of a federal trademark registration is ten years, with ten-year renewal terms. However, between the fifth and sixth year after the date of initial registration, the registrant must file an affidavit setting forth certain information to keep the registration alive. If no affidavit is filed, the registration is canceled.

The Importance of Trademarks

FDNY is the symbol of the New York City Fire Department. After the events of 9/11 the FDNY symbol was seen in hundreds of media reports. As the popularity of the symbol grew, many wanted to wear the symbol as a sign of solidarity with the citizens of New York City. FDNY appeared on hats, jackets, and T-shirts sold by hundreds of vendors throughout the United States.

But most of the sportswear that was sold with the FDNY initials was not licensed by the city of New York. The city held an unregistered trademark on the FDNY logo, but not a penny of profit from the sale of these unlicensed goods went to New York City. Amid the tragedy of the World Trade Center attacks, the city tried to manage and protect what was suddenly a million-dollar trademark.

People who did not know that the FDNY logo is a trademark were producing many of the goods being sold. To make the producers of these illegal goods aware of the trademark, New York City sent dozens of cease and desist letters to retailers who were known to be selling the illegal goods. The city then signed a licensing agreement with Macy's Department Stores, valued at $20 million, to be the sole licenser of FDNY products.

This is but one example of the value of owning a trademark. The primary confusion in the minds of many relates to what types of protection apply to a given thing. It's not unusual to hear of somebody stating that they are in the process of "patenting a name" or "copyrighting a slogan." Some manufacturers and inventors deliberately use this confusion to their advantage. For example, the Monopoly board game carries a copyright symbol on its box. This does not mean that the game is copyrighted. The artwork on the box is copyrighted. The game itself is patented. The name "Monopoly" is a trademark.

A Brief History of Trademarks

From earliest times humans have used marks to designate ownership. Primitive humans used marks to show ownership of animals, since as early as 5000 BC cave drawings show animals with symbols on their flanks. Marks have been found on commodities in Mesopotamia from around 3500 BC, and about 3000 BC marks were used commonly on items such as pottery in Egypt. Artisans in the Roman Empire pressed trademarks on bricks from 500 BC to AD 500.

During the Renaissance the use of marks changed. Marks began to be used not to identify the artisan or owner but to protect the consumer and show the quality of goods. The reason for this change was the rapid growth of guilds in the twelfth century. Marks protected the monopoly of the guild in a given industry. At a time when advertising was considered an unfair advantage, a guild's reputation was carried with its mark. The earliest English law on trademarks was the Bakers Marketing Law, which allowed bakers to stamp a mark on their bread.

During the thirteenth century, various laws protected cutlers' knives, bottle makers, and leather goods. In 1452 the earliest litigation over marks appeared in England, allowing a widow permission to use her husband's mark, and the seventeenth century saw court cases such as *Southern v. Howe*, in which a clothier's mark was infringed upon by a maker of inferior cloth. Also in the seventeenth century, porcelain marks were established in Holland, inspired by the marks on Chinese ceramics.

By the time the U.S. Constitution was written, trademarks were a commonly known method of identifying goods. The scant legislation at the time protected only goods being exported to other nations. Only individual state laws protected items manufactured within a state, with no provision for interstate commerce. It wasn't until 1870 that trademark legislation was passed based on the patent and trademark clause, Article 1, Section 8, of the Constitution. The first U.S. federal trademark was registered to Averill Paints in 1870. Two years later the first *Official Gazette* was published, listing weekly the trademarks granted by the U.S. government.

At the start of the twentieth century, companies trying to protect their established trademarks pressed for a new trademark law. In 1904 the Patent Office received 2,524 applications for trademarks. In 1905 a new trademark act gave new strength to trademarks, resulting in a rush to register marks. There were 16,224 marks filed for registration in 1905, and 415 of those still exist, including Vaseline, Pillsbury, and Singer.

The Lanham Act and the Trademark Law Revision Act

The basis for the current trademark law is the Lanham Act, passed in 1946. The Lanham Act is sixty years old and has shown the power to adapt to changing technologies with only minor adjustments. The most significant change to trademarks in the digital age affects the manner in which trademarks are searched and registered but not the basic concepts of trademark protection. For example, trademarks can now be searched online rather than manually, and it is now possible to register the mark online rather than on paper forms. (See chapter 6, "Searching Trademarks.")

In 1967 trademarks received a well-deserved boost in status when Congress changed the name of the Patent Office to the Patent and Trademark Office. Congress believed that in light of the office's responsibility for administering both patents and trademarks, the name Patent Office was misleading.

The Trademark Law Revision Act (TLRA) passed in 1988 contained a number of amendments to the Lanham Act. Previously a federal trademark had to be used in interstate commerce before it could be registered. The TLRA made prior registration possible. To confront the problem posed by the volume of abandoned or inactive marks ("deadwood") on the trademark register, the duration and renewal periods for the registration of a mark were reduced from twenty to ten years.

Controversies That Illustrate Trademark Concepts

One of the more interesting concepts in trademark law is the refusal to grant protection on marks that are considered immoral, scandalous, or deceptive. Since the interpretation of immorality is vague, some interesting challenges to trademarks have arisen. One of the more interesting examples of an "immoral" mark concerns Procter and Gamble's (P&G's) moon and stars trademark. P&G's trademark originated in 1851, when many products did not carry a brand name. The original trademark was a star that identified P&G candles, called Star Brand candles. The star became thirteen stars to symbolize the thirteen original colonies, and a man in the moon looking out on the night sky was added. The trademark was officially registered with the Patent Office in 1882.

One hundred years later, in 1981, a rumor began that alleged that the trademark is a symbol of satanism. Since satanism, in the view of some, is an immoral thing, there was a call by some religious groups for P&G to discontinue its trademark in accord with the "immoral, scandalous, or deceptive" provision in the Lanham Act. The story goes that a Procter and Gamble executive discussed satanism on a nationally televised talk show, thus starting the rumor that P&G was somehow linked with satanism.

The rumors were shown to be false. Producers for the TV programs mentioned in connection with the rumor confirmed that no one from P&G had ever appeared on their programs. Several nationally prominent religious leaders also called for an end to the false stories, calling the rumors vicious and ludicrous. Procter and Gamble filed over a dozen lawsuits in an attempt to resolve the matter, but the situation still resurfaces from time to time.

Trademarks can be lost if the trademark falls into common usage. The classic example of this is the trademark Kleenex. Although Kimberly-Clark, the owner of the trademark, still attempts to protect its trademark, the general public refers to all paper facial tissues as "kleenex." In the media, however, facial tissues cannot be referred to as "kleenex" unless they are Kleenex brand tissues. Corporations spend many millions of dollars annually protecting their trademarks against those who attempt to bring them into common usage. Here is a listing of registered trademarks that are in common usage or are tending to fall into common usage because the trademark name has become a generic term: Aspirin, Band-Aid, Dumpster, Frisbee, Hula Hoop, Jacuzzi, Popsicle, and Rollerblades.

Internet domain names are trademarks. In 1995 the Internet Entertainment Group (IEG) paid $20,000 to acquire the domain name candyland.com. Candyland .com was a sexually explicit Internet site. IEG spent an additional $150,000 to advertise the website in adult publications. In 1996 Hasbro, a world leader in children's toys and the owner of the trademark Candy Land for a children's board game, sued IEG. The Lanham Act permits the issuance of an injunction to prevent the "dilution or tarnishment" of a popular trademark. Hasbro maintained that using "Candyland" in association with a pornographic Internet site tarnished the wholesome imagery associated with Hasbro's Candy Land trademark and was likely to damage the positive associations evoked by use of the mark.

IEG maintained that it was not in the same industry as Hasbro. According to federal statute, similar trademarks are permitted if the industries in which the trademark holders operate are dissimilar. IEG pointed out that Candyland is a trademark in a wide variety of goods and services, including food, dolls, child care, clothing, retail grocery stores, vending machines, paper goods, wedding supplies, and real estate services. Indeed, at the time there were twenty-three trademark applications and fifty-nine unregistered uses of Candyland or Candy Land.

But the bigger issue in this case was that Hasbro was about to launch a new interactive division that would feature computer-oriented games and entertainment products. As one of Hasbro's popular products, Candy Land would be an integral part of its interactive strategy. Hasbro had planned to make the Candy Land game available online in a format that would allow children to play the game with other children around the world over the Internet. The thought of children typing in "Candyland" hoping to play this game and getting instead a pornographic website gave Hasbro executives nightmares.

IEG had spent over $700,000 to develop its Candyland site, but in the end Hasbro prevailed. In 1996 a federal court ruled that IEG had to give up the Candyland name, and the company was given six months to post notification at the URL to refer people to a differently named site.

Over the past ten years, colleges and universities have come to realize that a school's name and mascot can be valuable as intellectual property in an era when every T-shirt is a walking advertisement. Annual nationwide licensing of college paraphernalia is estimated at $2.5 billion. (Licensing simply gives a company the right to use a trademark owned by some other person or organization.) Penn State University, in reaction to the pirating of many different "official" Penn State logos, changed and trademarked its Nittany Lion logo in the mid-1990s. By registering a trademark on the new lion logo, Penn State was able to control others' marketing items that had some variation of the Nittany Lion, which is said to be the most recognized university mascot in the world. For over fifty years, with many subtle changes in the lion design, almost any version of the Nittany Lion statue represented Penn State, and marketers sold bootlegged Nittany Lion items openly. But with the new registered trademark design, the university had the strength of the federal government backing its right to be the sole marketer and licenser of Nittany Lion items.

In all of these examples one thing is true: a trademark, while only a word or a symbol, is valuable—so valuable that parties will spend a lot of money to defend their right to exclusively use it on their goods or services. Not only are trademarks strenuously protected, but any word or symbol that approximates a registered trademark is also cause for concern.

Domain Names

A domain name is part of a uniform resource locator (URL) on the Internet. A domain name can be a trademark—or it cannot be a trademark. At a basic level, the URL is the address of a site or a document on the Internet. A URL consists of a second-level domain, a "dot," and a top-level domain (TLD). The wording to the left of the dot is the second-level domain; the wording to the right of the dot is the TLD. For example, abc.com is a URL comprising a top-level domain, "com," and a second-level domain, "abc." URLs are usually preceded by http://www. So a URL may be http://www.abc.com, while the domain name may simply be abc.com.

In order to protect domain names and to ensure that a domain name does not duplicate another, domain names are registered. The registration of domain names is not done through the PTO but through one of two registering groups. The Internet Council of Registrars (CORE) and the Internet Corporation for Assigned Names and Numbers (ICANN) register domain names through hundreds of organizations called domain name registrars. A list of these registrars can be obtained at www .newregistrars.com. There is a fee involved, usually $70, but notification of whether a proposed domain name will be permitted is rapid, usually a matter of seconds, since all registrars use the same database of registered domain names. This will tell whether a domain name is registered, but it will not tell who owns the domain name. To see who owns a domain name, go to www.networksolutions.com/whois/.

This simple registration of domain names became a thriving cottage industry in the 1990s, in a practice that became known as "cybersquatting." Entrepreneurs began to register every domain name that potentially would have economic value, such as the names of well-known corporations or their products. Then when the actual company—which was late in realizing the potential of the Internet—wanted to register a domain name bearing its name or products, the registrant would discover that the domain name was already registered by another. In order to obtain that domain name, the registrant would have to pay off the holder of the domain name at inflated prices.

A variant of this practice is known as "typosquatting." This is the practice of a domain name similar to an existing domain name being registered by a person who is not associated with the original company in order to attract surfers who may misspell a URL or not type the correct URL. To lessen this risk, some companies deliberately buy up similar domain names. To see this in action, type in "googel.com" or "gogle.com" in a browser's URL box. Both misspellings take the surfer to Google's home page. This preventive measure is not perfect, however, since typing in "googles.com" leads to a children's website. Googles are alien creatures from a children's book, and the domain name was registered in July 1997, two months before Google registered its domain name as a trademark.

In the early days of domain name registration, some people bought up nonsense names, misspellings of popular companies, and almost any variation on any word in hopes of later selling the domain name to a legitimate company that was trying to protect itself against typosquatting. Another variation of cybersquatting is seen in "fan sites" such as beatlesrule.com or "antifan sites" such as beatlesstink.com. When companies register domain names they also register as many variations on the name of the domain as is possible, including variations such as .org or .biz.

If a registered domain name is being used by a company or individual, can it also be registered as a trademark? Yes. First, the prospective trademark has to consist of only the domain name and not the entire URL. Second, the domain name has to be used to identify goods and services and not only act as an address to an Internet site. There are many good examples of this. Amazon.com is one of them. Amazon.com is not only the address of the Internet site but is a symbol of the various goods and services sold on the site. Amazon.com is also the name of the company that operates the Internet site and the name under which its stock is traded.

To register a domain name as a trademark, it has to first be registered by CORE or ICANN as a domain name. Then the domain name has to act as an identifier of goods and services and not only act as part of a URL. From there on, the registration process is the same as for any other trademark.

Questions and Answers about Trademarks

Q   What is a trademark?

A   A trademark is a word, phrase, symbol, design, or combination of words, phrases, symbols, or designs that identifies and distinguishes the source of goods or services of one party from those of another.

Q   What is a service mark?

A   A service mark is a trademark, except that it identifies a service rather than goods.

Q   Are advertising slogans, written statements on T-shirts, or bumper sticker sayings, such as Nike's "Just Do It," protected by copyright or trademark?

A   Copyright is reserved for prose, poetry, artistic works, computer programs, movies, and the like. One cannot copyright a saying or slogan. Advertising slogans are trademarks.

Q   If a person sees a product that is trademarked in France, can he get the U.S. trademark on it?

A   Only if he owns the French trademark. Only the true owner has the right to trademark in other countries, according to international trademark treaties and agreements.

Q   So a person cannot trademark the French product. He decides to go ahead and use the mark in the United States anyway. Can the French owner stop him?

A   No, unless the French owner has also registered that trademark in the United States. A trademark is enforceable only within the country in which it was issued. See the International Trademark Association (www.inta.org) for guidance.

Q   Those seeking trademark protection often mail themselves a drawing and description of their trademark by certified mail. Is this a good way to protect trademark rights?

A   No. Certified mailers are poor substitutes for a federally registered trademark, although some attorneys still recommend this method of protection for their clients.

Q   Does one have to wait until a trademark registration is granted before a trademark can be used?

A   No. In fact, a mark has to be used first on goods or services before one can apply for registration, or else one must file an application showing intent to use it.

Q   Does the symbol ® mean the same thing as the symbol ™?

A   No. The ® symbol means that the trademark is federally registered. The ™ symbol means that the mark is being claimed as a trademark but is not federally registered.

Q   After the initial ten-year protection period for a trademark, can a trademark be renewed?

A   Yes. Trademarks can be renewed for indefinite ten-year periods as long as evidence is shown that the mark is still in use.

Q   If a trademark isn't labeled ®, can another use it, since the law requires trademarks to be identified?

A   No. One does not need to use the ® symbol in order to provide notice of trademark rights. One may also use the phrases "Reg. U.S. Pat. & Tm. Off." or "Registered in the U.S. Patent and Trademark Office" or not identify the trademark registration in any way. However, it is illegal to use the ® symbol if the mark is not federally registered.

Q   After receiving a trademark, can it be declared invalid or taken away?

A   A trademark can be canceled for many reasons. To cancel a trademark, one has to file a petition with the PTO. A "petition to cancel" is a lawsuit within the PTO. See www.usip.com/articles/costcons.htm.

Q   If somebody infringes on a trademark, can the owner file a report with the PTO so that the PTO will take action against the infringer?

A   No. The PTO is not a law enforcement agency. The trademark owner alone is responsible for protecting her rights.

Q   Is it true that words like Kleenex and Thermos were once trademarks but are now generic terms, allowing anybody to use them on goods?

A   These terms are still valid trademarks, but their common usage makes them difficult to protect. Xerox went through an extensive campaign several years ago to remind people that Xerox was not a generic term.

Q   If one changes one or two letters of a trademark in use, for example, changing Xerox to Zeroks, can one use the changed mark on goods without infringing on an existing trademark?

A   No. A trademark has to be different enough to avoid confusion, mistake, or deception. Usually changing one or two letters is not enough.

Q   Is a trademark a graphic symbol, while a trade name is a word?

A   A trade name is a type of trademark that comprises wording only. A trademark is any word, symbol, or sound used to identify goods.

Q   Before a trademark is issued, does the PTO go through an extensive search, in much the same way as the PTO does for patents?

A   Yes, and the trademark applicant can save time and money by doing her own search before paying trademark application fees.

Q   A person invents an electric fork and attempts to trademark it with the name "Electric Fork." Can one do this?

A   No. A product's common descriptive name, even if its function is unique, cannot be protected. See www.lfiplaw.com/trademarks.htm.

Q   Is the PTO the only place to register a trademark?

A   Although application forms are available at various online sites, the PTO is the only office that can accept domestic applications and issue registrations. Recently, the PTO has allowed trademark application online.

Q   Should a person do a trademark search herself or use one of the fee-based services?

A   If a person feels comfortable with searching trademarks after reading the chapter in this book on trademark searching, they should attempt it. If not comfortable, a trademark attorney or a fee-based service would be appropriate. Be warned, most trademark search services are reputable and professional, but a few are not. Be cautious about selecting a fee-based service.

Q   Who can own a U.S. trademark?

A   Any person regardless of age or U.S. citizenship can own a U.S. trademark. Corporations and partnerships can own trademarks. State laws differ in that they regulate who may establish a business in a given state and determine restrictions on the age of a mark owner.

Q   Can one copyright or trademark a name, title, slogan, or logo?

A   Copyright does not protect names, titles, slogans, or short phrases. In some cases, these things may be protected as trademarks. Copyright protection may be available for trademark artwork, and in some circumstances an artistic logo may also be protected as a trademark.

Q   How long does it take to get a trademark?

A   The time the PTO requires to process an application varies depending on the amount of material that the office is receiving. One may generally expect a certificate of registration within approximately eight months of submission.

Q   Is there a list of trademarks that are in the public domain?

A   No. A public domain trademark would defeat the whole purpose of a trademark. The only exceptions to proprietary trademarks would be government shields or logos such as the shield for the U.S. Department of Commerce or the FBI. However, using these on goods or services if one is not representing that governmental branch may create other legal problems.

Q   Does a trademark have to be registered with the PTO to be protected?

A   No. Registration is voluntary. But having a registered trademark carries weight in any legal action involving interstate commerce and has many other advantages.

Q   How does one register a trademark?

A   To register a trademark, one needs to submit a completed application form, a drawing of the mark, a nonrefundable filing fee of $345, and specimens showing the use of the trademark in commerce.

Q Can one make photocopies of the application form rather than using an original form?

A Yes, one can make copies of trademark forms if they meet the following criteria: they must be photocopied back-to-back and head-to-head on a single sheet of 8½-by-11-inch white paper. In other words, your copy must look just like the original. Facsimile copies available online are also acceptable, as is printing out an online application form and mailing it to the PTO. However, the PTO is moving away from paper applications and encourages application online through its website at www.uspto.gov.

Q May one register more than one mark on the same application?

A No. One mark per application.

Q Can one renew a trademark?

A Yes. A trademark lasts ten years, but between the fifth and sixth year following registration, a renewal has to be submitted showing that the trademark is still in use. Trademarks may be renewed in perpetuity.

Q Can one submit an application online?

A Yes. Go to www.uspto.gov and click the "Trademarks" link. There is a link to TEAS, the Trademark Electronic Application System. From this page one can submit an application online, or one can fill out forms online, print them out, and mail them to the PTO.

Q Can foreigners register a trademark in the United States?

A Yes. According to treaty agreements with other nations, a trademark that is used in another country can also be registered in the United States as long as the registrant is the holder of the foreign trademark.

Q Can a minor register a trademark?

A Yes. There is no age requirement for registering a trademark; however, state laws may regulate business dealings involving minors. For information on relevant state laws, consult an attorney.

Q Does a person have to use his or her real name on the application?

A The application is filed using the name of the owner of the mark. This may be an individual, a partnership, a corporation, or an association. If an individual files using a pseudonym, that name must be one with which the applicant does business and not one used simply to remain anonymous on the application. Normally, these types of anonymous or fictitious names are announced publicly in the "legal notices" sections of local or national newspapers.

Q Are trademarks transferable?

A Yes. Like any other property, the owner may transfer all or part of the rights to another.

Q   Can one trademark the name of a band or musical group?

A   Yes. Some names may be protected under trademark law.

Q   How much different does a trademark have to be from an existing trademark to register a new trademark?

A   One may register a new trademark if the changes are substantial and do not cause confusion in the mind of the consumer. Chapter 1 contains examples of legal actions concerning similar trademarks. Simply making spelling changes does not warrant a new registration; for example, attempting to register Zeroks as a trademark for photocopiers would be questionable.

Q   What is a trademark notice? How does one put a trademark notice on one's products?

A   A trademark notice is an identifier placed on copies of a product to inform consumers of trademark ownership. There are three commonly used symbols: ®, ™, and ℠. The ™ symbol is used on products, and the ℠ symbol is used on services to alert the public of the owner's claim to the mark the symbol is attached to. These symbols denote marks for which rights are claimed but that are not registered trademarks. By contrast, the ® symbol means that the mark to which it is attached is a registered trademark. None of the marks are required by law, and they only serve as notice of the owner's claim to the mark, registered or not. However, it is illegal to use the ® symbol unless the trademark to which it is attached is federally registered.

Q   Somebody infringed on a trademark. What can the damaged party do?

A   A party may seek to protect his trademark against unauthorized use by filing a civil lawsuit in a federal district court. If one believes that a trademark has been infringed upon, one should consult an attorney. In cases of willful infringement for profit, the U.S. attorney may initiate a criminal investigation.

Q   Is a trademark good in other countries?

A   The United States has trademark treaties and agreements with more than 100 countries throughout the world, and as a result of these agreements, the United States honors other countries' trademarks and vice versa. But a U.S. trademark is not valid in other countries. A trademark owner would have to register that mark in a given country under its laws. The treaties only give the original owner of the mark the right to register it in other countries rather than having the existing U.S. mark registered in another country by another party. However, the United States does not have such trademark relationships with every country.

Q   How does one get permission to use somebody else's trademark?

A   If one is not certain about the ownership of a mark or has other related questions, one can conduct a search of registered trademarks or have an attorney do this. See chapter 6 in this book. One should bear in mind that others will not license a successful trademark that is in current use for use on other products. Only trademarks that are still current but not in current use are logical licensing candidates.

Q   Could one be sued for using somebody else's trademark?

A   If someone uses a trademark without authorization, the owner may be entitled to bring an infringement action against that party. Penalties for infringement on a trademark range from $5,000 for each violation to well over $1 million.

Q   If a person uses only part of a trademark, for example, only the face of the Quaker on the Quaker Oats box and not the entire mark with the Quaker wearing a hat in a circle with the words "Old Fashioned" underneath the hat, can that portion be used as part of another mark?

A   No. Not only does a new mark have to be original, but it must also not even be similar to an existing mark. See chapter 1 for examples of infringing marks.

Q   A student doing a multimedia art project uses the Quaker Oats trademark to illustrate Quaker dress. She submits this project to a national competition for classroom multimedia projects. Is she in violation of trademark law?

A   Generally no, as long as the competition was expressly for classroom work by students. The student was not seeking profit and was not confusing the public by intending to show that Quaker Oats owned or was responsible for the project. However, use of others' marks is a slippery area. See chapter 1 for examples of trademark controversies.

Searching
Trademarks

Before applying for a trademark, an applicant is advised to search existing registered, common law, and pending trademarks in order to determine whether the mark they intend to register has already been registered by another party. The Patent and Trademark Office will perform an exhaustive search before approving an application, so some applicants skip this crucial step when making a trademark application. It is not necessary for an applicant to perform a search, but it is prudent, since an applicant would forfeit all application fees and the time spent preparing the application if their mark is found to have already been registered by another party. The cost of a basic search is less than the expense of changing a mark already in use or refiling an application. Additionally, librarians need to know how to search a mark in order to assist those seeking information such as the owner of a mark or the exact wording or design of an existing mark.

Even if an exact match of a trademark is not found, the PTO determines whether there would be likelihood of confusion between two similar marks, that is, whether consumers would be likely to associate the goods or services of one party with those of another party as a result of the use of the marks at issue. The principal factors to be considered in reaching this decision are the similarity of the marks and the commercial relationship between the goods and services identified by the marks. This means that similar marks may be used in different industries as long as there is no confusion in the mind of the consumer. For example, the trademark Macintosh may be registered to a manufacturer of raincoats, and to an apple grower, and it may also be the registered trademark for a company that makes personal computers.

Six

Examples of Infringing Marks

Below are two groups of trademarks to show how difficult it is to determine which marks may be infringing on the other. In one group of trademark pairs, the two marks presented were determined to be infringing marks. In the other set, the marks were determined not to be infringing marks. In List 1, the marks were considered to be so similar as to confuse the consumer. The marks in List 2 were allowed to coexist as registered trademarks. The primary determining factor is whether the two similar marks are being used in the same type of industry. If they are used in different industries, similar marks are usually permitted.

List 1: Nonpermitted Similar Trademarks

Ameribanc and Bank of America

Blockbuster Video and Video Buster

Century 21 and Century 31

Datsun and Dotson

Good Morning and Buenos Días

Listerine and Listogen

Miracle Whip and Salad Whip

Philadelphia and Pennsylvania

S.O. and Esso

Toys "R" Us and Kids "R" Us

List 2: Permitted Similar Trademarks

Boston Tea Party and Boston Sea Party

Car-X and Exxon

Fruit of the Loom and Fruit of the Earth

Hour after Hour and Shower to Shower

Marshall Field's and Mrs. Fields

Silky Touch and Touch O'Silk

T.G.I. Friday's and E.L. Saturday's

Vantage and Advance

Overview of the Search Process

As an overview of the entire process, the following are the standard steps necessary to complete a trademark search. For this book, these steps will be altered somewhat, but an understanding of what a traditional mark search looks like is helpful. The full search process recommended in this book is described in detail later in this chapter.

1. Goods and Services Manual. Go to the PTO website at www.uspto.gov and click on the "Trademarks" link. Then click on "Identification Manual." You should begin with this alphabetical listing of acceptable terms for the identification of goods and services. Locate terms that describe your good or service. For example, "flying discs" is the acceptable term for a flying saucer–type toy. Note the international class number listed next to each term. Also identify terms for goods or services that are used, advertised, or sold with your product. For instance, peanut butter is sold and used with jellies and jams. This manual is located at **www.uspto.gov > Trademarks > Identification Manual.**

2. International Schedule of Classes, or International Classification. Scan this schedule for additional classes that are related to your product or service. For instance, if your product is income-tax preparation software, class 36 would be related because it includes services related to insurance, financial affairs, monetary affairs, and real estate. The classification schedule is given in the next section of this chapter.

3. Trademark Manual of Examining Procedure (TMEP). Review chapter 1400 of this manual for the appropriate class scope notes in order to confirm the terms and classes you have chosen. For example, class 8 (Hand tools) includes cutlery but not surgical knives, which are in class 10 (Medical apparatus), or fencing weapons, which are found in class 28 (Toys and sporting goods). The manual is located at **www.uspto.gov > Trademarks > Manual Examining Procedure.**

4. Design Search Code Manual. If your mark incorporates a design or logo, you must search for trademarks that might be confusingly similar to it. Use the index at the back of the Design Search Code Manual to locate the appropriate six-digit code for each design element in your mark. For example, a logo depicting an eagle would be coded 03.15.01. Each element in a logo is assigned a design code. Carefully review the guidelines in each category. This manual is located at **www.uspto.gov > Trademarks > Other Guides and Manuals > Design Search Code Manual.**

5. Trademarks Registered and Pending. Conduct the search combining your word, mark, or logo with the terms, classes, and design codes you've identified in Steps 1–4. Remember to search for alternate spellings, phonetic and foreign language equivalents, and synonyms and homonyms, for example, Sno Brite, Snow Bright, Snow-Brite, Sno-Bright, Snow White, and so on. This search is conducted at **www.uspto.gov > Trademarks > Search Trademarks.**

6. TARR Trademark Status Database. Finally, check TARR, the Trademark Applications and Registrations Retrieval system, for the current status of the marks you found in Step 5. Records in the web trademark databases are linked directly to their TARR equivalents. The TARR database is updated daily at 5 a.m. and contains important trademark application and registration information not found in the *Official Gazette*. The database is located at **www.uspto.gov > Trademarks > Check Status.**

Trademark Classification

Like patents, trademarks are arranged by categories. Fortunately, there are fewer trademark categories than there are patent classifications. There are over 400 patent classifications, while there are only 42 trademark classifications in the International Schedule of Classes (or International Classification), which is given below.

Goods

Class 1 (Chemicals). Chemicals used in industry, science, and photography, as well as in agriculture, horticulture, and forestry; unprocessed artificial resins, unprocessed plastics; manures; fire-extinguishing compositions; tempering and soldering preparations; chemical substances for preserving foodstuffs; tanning substances; adhesives used in industry.

Class 2 (Paints). Paints, varnishes, lacquers; preservatives against rust and against deterioration of wood; colorants; mordants; raw natural resins; metals in foil and powder form for painters, decorators, printers, and artists.

Class 3 (Cosmetics and cleaning preparations). Bleaching preparations and other substances for laundry use; cleaning, polishing, scouring, and abrasive preparations; soaps; perfumery, essential oils, cosmetics, hair lotions; dentifrices.

Class 4 (Lubricants and fuels). Industrial oils and greases; lubricants; dust-absorbing, wetting, and binding compositions; fuels (including motor spirit) and illuminants; candles, wicks.

Class 5 (Pharmaceuticals). Pharmaceutical, veterinary, and sanitary preparations; dietetic substances adapted for medical use, food for babies; plasters, materials for dressings; material for stopping teeth, dental wax; disinfectants; preparations for destroying vermin; fungicides, herbicides.

Class 6 (Metal goods). Common metals and their alloys; metal building materials; transportable buildings of metal; materials of metal for railway tracks; non-electric cables and wires of common metal; ironmongery, small items of metal hardware; pipes and tubes of metal; safes; goods of common metal not included in other classes; ores.

Class 7 (Machinery). Machines and machine tools; motors and engines (except for land vehicles); machine coupling and transmission components (except for land vehicles); agricultural implements; incubators for eggs.

Class 8 (Hand tools). Hand tools and implements (hand-operated); cutlery; side arms; razors.

Class 9 (Electrical and scientific apparatus). Scientific, nautical, surveying, electric, photographic, cinematographic, optical, weighing, measuring, signaling, checking (supervision), life-saving, and teaching apparatus and instruments;

apparatus for recording, transmission, or reproduction of sound or images; magnetic data carriers, recording discs; automatic vending machines and mechanisms for coin-operated apparatus; cash registers, calculating machines, data-processing equipment and computers; fire-extinguishing apparatus.

Class 10 (Medical apparatus). Surgical, medical, dental, and veterinary apparatus and instruments; artificial limbs, eyes, and teeth; orthopedic articles; suture materials.

Class 11 (Environmental control apparatus). Apparatus for lighting, heating, steam generating, cooking, refrigerating, drying, ventilating, water supply, and sanitary purposes.

Class 12 (Vehicles). Vehicles; apparatus for locomotion by land, air, or water.

Class 13 (Firearms). Firearms; ammunition and projectiles; explosives; fireworks.

Class 14 (Jewelry). Precious metals and their alloys and goods in precious metals or coated therewith, not included in other classes; jewelry, precious stones; horological and chronometric instruments.

Class 15 (Musical instruments). Musical instruments.

Class 16 (Paper goods and printed matter). Paper, cardboard, and goods made from these materials, not included in other classes; printed matter; book-binding material; photographs; stationery; adhesives for stationery or household purposes; artists' materials; paint brushes; typewriters and office requisites (except furniture); instructional and teaching material (except apparatus); plastic material for packaging (not included in other classes); playing cards; printers' type; printing blocks.

Class 17 (Rubber goods). Rubber, gutta-percha, gum, asbestos, mica, and goods made from these materials and not included in other classes; plastics in extruded form for use in manufacture; packing, stopping, and insulating materials; flexible pipes, not of metal.

Class 18 (Leather goods). Leather and imitations of leather, and goods made of these materials and not included in other classes; animal skins, hides; trunks and traveling bags; umbrellas, parasols, and walking sticks; whips, harness, and saddlery.

Class 19 (Non-metallic building materials). Building materials (non-metallic); non-metallic rigid pipes for building; asphalt, pitch, and bitumen; non-metallic transportable buildings; monuments, not of metal.

Class 20 (Furniture and articles not otherwise classified). Furniture, mirrors, picture frames; goods (not included in other classes) of wood, cork, reed, cane, wicker, horn, bone, ivory, whalebone, shell, amber, mother-of-pearl, meerschaum, and substitutes for all these materials, or of plastics.

Class 21 (Housewares and glass). Household or kitchen utensils and containers (not of precious metal or coated therewith); combs and sponges; brushes (except paint brushes); brush-making materials; articles for cleaning purposes; steel wool; unworked or semi-worked glass (except glass used in building); glassware, porcelain, and earthenware not included in other classes.

Class 22 (Cordage and fibers). Ropes, string, nets, tents, awnings, tarpaulins, sails, sacks, and bags (not included in other classes); padding and stuffing materials (except of rubber or plastics); raw fibrous textile materials.

Class 23 (Yarns and threads). Yarns and threads, for textile use.

Class 24 (Fabrics). Textiles and textile goods, not included in other classes; bed and table covers.

Class 25 (Clothing). Clothing, footwear, headgear.

Class 26 (Fancy goods). Lace and embroidery, ribbons, and braid; buttons, hooks and eyes, pins and needles; artificial flowers.

Class 27 (Floor coverings). Carpets, rugs, mats and matting, linoleum, and other materials for covering existing floors; wall hangings (non-textile).

Class 28 (Toys and sporting goods). Games and playthings; gymnastic and sporting articles not included in other classes; decorations for Christmas trees.

Class 29 (Meats and processed foods). Meat, fish, poultry, and game; meat extracts; preserved, dried, and cooked fruits and vegetables; jellies, jams, fruit sauces; eggs, milk, and milk products; edible oils and fats.

Class 30 (Staple foods). Coffee, tea, cocoa, sugar, rice, tapioca, sago, artificial coffee; flour and preparations made from cereals, bread, pastry and confectionery, spices, honey, treacle; yeast, baking powder, salt, mustard; vinegar, sauces (condiments); ice.

Class 31 (Natural agricultural products). Agricultural, horticultural, and forestry products and grains not included in other classes; live animals; fresh fruits and vegetables; seeds, natural plants, and flowers; foodstuffs for animals, malt.

Class 32 (Light beverages). Beers; mineral and aerated waters and other non-alcoholic drinks; fruit drinks and fruit juices; syrups and other preparations for making beverages.

Class 33 (Wines and spirits). Alcoholic beverages (except beers).

Class 34 (Smokers' articles). Tobacco; smokers' articles; matches.

Services

Class 35 (Advertising and business services). Advertising; business management; business administration; office functions.

Class 36 (Insurance and financial services). Insurance; financial affairs; monetary affairs; real estate affairs.

Class 37 (Construction and repair services). Building construction; repair; installation services.

Class 38 (Communication services). Telecommunications.

Class 39 (Transportation and storage services). Transport; packaging and storage of goods; travel arrangement.

Class 40 (Material treatment services). Treatment of materials.

Class 41 (Education and entertainment services). Education; providing of training; entertainment; sporting and cultural activities.

Class 42 (Miscellaneous services). Providing of food and drink; temporary accommodation; medical, hygienic, and beauty care; veterinary and agricultural services; legal services; scientific and industrial research; computer programming; services that cannot be placed in other classes.

Beginning the Search

There is a problem that arises from this reduction in the number of classifications: if searching for a graphic symbol rather than a word or phrase, a searcher will have to search classification areas that categorize symbols by type. This can be a difficult process. By far, a word search is easier than a search for a graphic symbol. The word search will be explained first in this chapter and then the more difficult symbol search.

There are a variety of ways to perform a search: by doing a search in the PTO Public Search Room in Arlington, Virginia; by visiting a Patent and Trademark Depository Library; by using various online resources; or by employing either a private trademark search company or an attorney who deals with trademark law. This book will cover only one method, an online method using the PTO website.

To search for trademark word names and phrases, one must first identify the proper category for the goods or services the trademark represents. By using the International Classification, which contains brief descriptions of what each class contains, one can select a proper class for a given trademark, but there is an easier way.

The sample search for this book is for "nike," which is a word trademark registered to Nike Corporation. Since Nike may be a trademark for sports equipment, sportswear, shoes, or many other items, the "nike" being searched is the Nike trademark for shoes. Begin by going to the PTO website: **www.uspto .gov > Trademarks > Search TM Database (TESS)**. The resulting page is shown in figure 6-1.

This is the search page. There are five kinds of searches that can be done: New User (also called Basic), Structured Form, Free Form, Dictionary, and Date. Simply

United States Patent and Trademark Office
Home | Site
Index | Search | FAQ | Glossary | Guides | Contacts | eBusiness | eBiz
alerts | News | Help

Are you filing electronically through TEAS?

Trademarks > Trademark Electronic Search System(Tess)

TESS was last updated on Fri Jan 26 04:18:59 EST 2007

HELP   **News!**

NOTE: Click **here** for a description of changes to word mark entries for standard character marks submitted via TEAS Plus that you may wish to consider when constructing your TESS searches.

Logout

Please logout when you are done to release system resources allocated for you.

Select The Search Form

▶ **New User Form Search (Basic)**

▶ **Structured Form Search (Boolean)**

▶ **Free Form Search (Advanced Search)**

▶ **Browse Dictionary (View Indexes)**

▶ **Search OG Publication Date or Registration Date**

Update Information: TESS contains more than 4 million pending, registered and dead federal trademarks. Select our **News!** button for the latest complete filing date available on TESS. On Tuesday through Saturday, TESS will not be available for one hour from 4:00 to 5:00AM (EST) for database update. *TESS was last updated on Fri Jan 26 04:18:59 EST 2007*
.

Important Notices Concerning TESS: TESS is intended for use by the general public. Due to limitations of equipment and bandwidth, TESS is not intended to be a source for bulk downloads of USPTO data. Bulk data may be purchased from USPTO at cost (see the **USPTO Products and Services Catalog**). Individuals, companies, IP addresses, or blocks of IP addresses who, in effect, deny service to the general public by generating unusually high

Figure 6-1

PTO website's "Trademark Search" page

enter a term in the "New User" search (or several related terms combined with AND, e.g., "just AND do AND it"). There are four other options for this type of word search, but the purpose of this chapter is to keep things simple. Enter "nike" and hit "Submit Query." The resulting page is shown in figure 6-2.

Keep in mind that as of this writing, the page displayed was accurate, but it could change frequently, since new Nike Corporation trademarks may be issued each Tuesday, and new "nike" trademarks would alter the listing shown. This is a real possibility, since as of December 2006 Nike held 637 trademarks in a variety of classifications.

There are several important pieces of information shown here. The serial numbers and the registration numbers are displayed. These are important if a searcher has one of these numbers that may have accompanied an existing mark. This way a mark can be searched directly; however, an amateur searcher normally doesn't have a serial number or registration number. The trademark word is displayed. This is what is matched in a New User search. The "Live or Dead" indicator is shown. This indicates whether the mark is still active or is no longer in use. If a mark is dead, it may be possible to use it on one's goods or services.

Click the first "nike" word mark listed, which is that single word and not "nike" combined with another word(s), serial number 78528705. The resulting page is shown in figure 6-3.

In the traditional searching steps shown earlier in "Overview of the Search Process," the first two steps were to identify the terms and the class for a given mark. The method of searching given here skips the first two steps of that procedure. This is done because the search demonstrated here is a New User search. Just entering the term to see if it comes up is easier than verifying first if it exists. If hits do result from a New User search, the International Classification (IC) is listed on the document; in this example, international class 009. This is simpler than first searching for an appropriate class. Of course, a searcher would have to have an existing trademark in mind to do this, but if searching for a trademark, most businesspeople know their competition and can enter the competitor's trademark to get the proper class.

On the document shown in figure 6-3, the IC is 009. This is the classification for electrical and scientific apparatus. The definition that is given shows that all types of measuring devices are included in this class, as well as vending machines, data-processing equipment, and computer software. If a searcher needs to verify this, she could go to the Trademark Manual of Examining Procedure in the traditional search steps shown earlier in the "Overview" and check if shoes belong in this class. Obviously shoes are not in this class.

By referring to the listing of goods and services in the International Classification above, one can locate shoes as being part of IC 025—the class for clothing, including shoes. Normally the proper IC for a good or service is apparent, but if the searcher does have difficulty, this method should be used to help identify a proper IC.

So a searcher knows that Nike does have a lot of trademarks, but without going through all of the trademarks listed in the New User search, how can the "nike" that is a mark for a shoe be located?

United States Patent and Trademark Office

Home | Site Index | Search | FAQ | Glossary | Guides | Contacts | eBusiness | eBiz alerts | News | Help

Trademarks > Trademark Electronic Search System(Tess)

TESS was last updated on Fri Jan 26 04:18:59 EST 2007

| TESS HOME | NEW USER | STRUCTURED | FREE FORM | BROWSE DICT | SEARCH OG | PREV LIST | NEXT LIST | BOTTOM | HELP |

Logout | *Please logout when you are done to release system resources allocated for you.*

Start | List At: [ ] OR Jump | to record: [ ]

120 Records(s) found (This page: 1 ~ 50)

Refine Search | (nike)[COMB] | Submit

Current Search: S1: (nike)[COMB] docs: 120 occ: 257

	Serial Number	Reg. Number	Word Mark	Check Status	Live/Dead
1	78856997		NIKE IHM	TARR	LIVE
2	78872655		NIKE LUNARLITE	TARR	LIVE
3	78848308		NIKE STABILFLEX	TARR	LIVE
4	78801040	3192901	NIKE FREE	TARR	LIVE
5	78872601		NIKE RECOVERY	TARR	LIVE
6	78613193	3087455	NIKEFREE	TARR	LIVE
7	78528705		NIKE	TARR	LIVE
8	78528586		NIKE	TARR	LIVE
9	78514158	3061272	NIKE MAXSIGHT	TARR	LIVE
10	78248500	3167342	NIKE	TARR	LIVE
11	78228984		NIKE VAULT	TARR	LIVE
12	78411705	3081688	NIKE	TARR	LIVE
13	78406612		NIKE SHOX	TARR	LIVE
14	78228986		NIKE VAULT	TARR	LIVE
15	78228981		NIKE VAULT	TARR	DEAD
16	78222686		NIKE GRIND	TARR	DEAD
17	78222041	2895300	NIKE GRIND	TARR	LIVE
18	78191038	2804865	NIKE SPHERE	TARR	LIVE
19	77078429		NIKEGOLF	TARR	LIVE
20	76337599		NIKE SPORTS DRINK	TARR	DEAD
21	76123346		NIKEPAL	TARR	LIVE
22	76088450		NIKE SHOX	TARR	DEAD
23	75980787	2480935	NIKE GRIND	TARR	LIVE

Figure 6-2

Results of a New User search: Nike trademarks

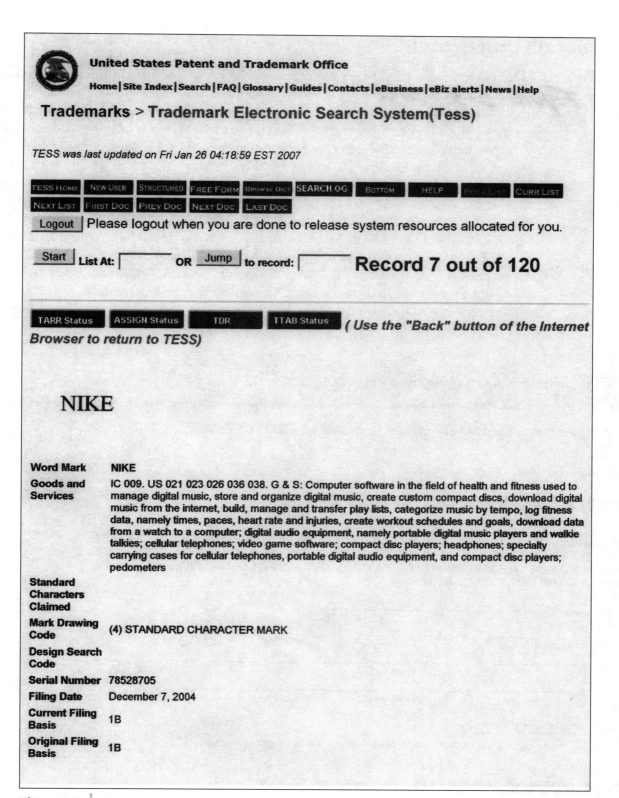

United States Patent and Trademark Office

Home | Site Index | Search | FAQ | Glossary | Guides | Contacts | eBusiness | eBiz alerts | News | Help

Trademarks > Trademark Electronic Search System(Tess)

TESS was last updated on Fri Jan 26 04:18:59 EST 2007

TESS HOME NEW USER STRUCTURED FREE FORM BROWSE DICT SEARCH OG BOTTOM HELP PREV LIST CURR LIST
NEXT LIST FIRST DOC PREV DOC NEXT DOC LAST DOC

Logout | Please logout when you are done to release system resources allocated for you.

Start | List At: [   ] OR Jump | to record: [   ] **Record 7 out of 120**

TARR Status ASSIGN Status TDR TTAB Status *(Use the "Back" button of the Internet Browser to return to TESS)*

NIKE

Word Mark	NIKE
Goods and Services	IC 009. US 021 023 026 036 038. G & S: Computer software in the field of health and fitness used to manage digital music, store and organize digital music, create custom compact discs, download digital music from the internet, build, manage and transfer play lists, categorize music by tempo, log fitness data, namely times, paces, heart rate and injuries, create workout schedules and goals, download data from a watch to a computer; digital audio equipment, namely portable digital music players and walkie talkies; cellular telephones; video game software; compact disc players; headphones; specialty carrying cases for cellular telephones, portable digital audio equipment, and compact disc players; pedometers
Standard Characters Claimed	
Mark Drawing Code	(4) STANDARD CHARACTER MARK
Design Search Code	
Serial Number	78528705
Filing Date	December 7, 2004
Current Filing Basis	1B
Original Filing Basis	1B

Figure 6-3

A Nike trademark

Structured Form Search

Go to the Structured Form search, the second option shown in figure 6-1, and click on it. The resulting page is shown in figure 6-4.

This type of search gives the flexibility to enter terms; link them to each other using the Boolean operators AND, OR, and NOT; or relate the words to each other with features such as NEAR or adjacent (ADJ). This type of search also lets a searcher look for terms in any field of the trademark record. Fields were shown in the first type of search when the single word "nike" trademark was displayed (see figure 6-3). Fields are things like serial number, filing date, type of mark, and so on.

If the Structured Form search strategy is used without designating a particular field to search—that is, "nike" in the top box of the search form and "shoes" in the second—the result totals more than 82,000 hits. It is important in this type of search to limit terms to a particular field. The only thing a searcher knows at this point from the New User search is that the mark is the word "nike" and it is in class 025, and it is owned by Nike Corporation in Beaverton, Oregon.

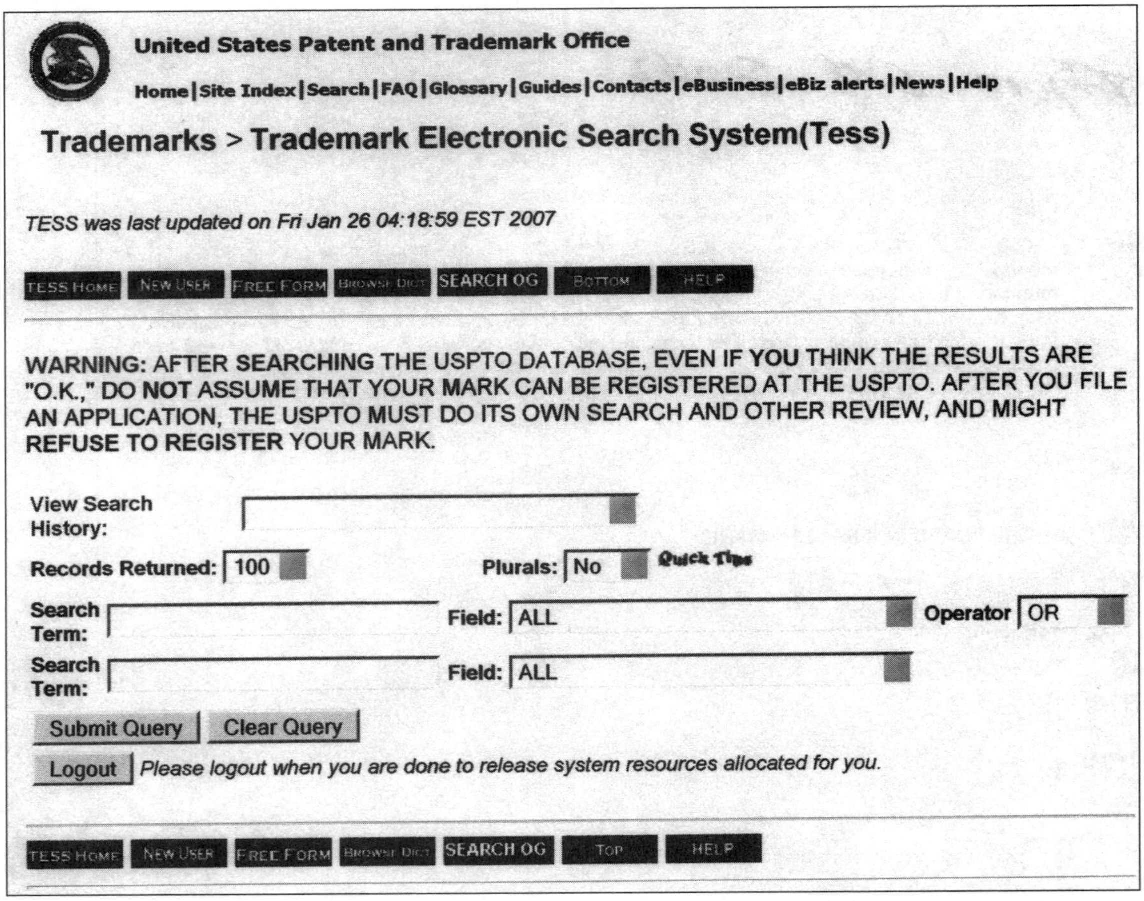

United States Patent and Trademark Office

Home | Site Index | Search | FAQ | Glossary | Guides | Contacts | eBusiness | eBiz alerts | News | Help

Trademarks > Trademark Electronic Search System(Tess)

TESS was last updated on Fri Jan 26 04:18:59 EST 2007

TESS HOME | NEW USER | FREE FORM | BROWSE DICT | SEARCH OG | BOTTOM | HELP

WARNING: AFTER SEARCHING THE USPTO DATABASE, EVEN IF YOU THINK THE RESULTS ARE "O.K.," DO NOT ASSUME THAT YOUR MARK CAN BE REGISTERED AT THE USPTO. AFTER YOU FILE AN APPLICATION, THE USPTO MUST DO ITS OWN SEARCH AND OTHER REVIEW, AND MIGHT REFUSE TO REGISTER YOUR MARK.

View Search History:

Records Returned: 100   Plurals: No   Quick Tips

Search Term: Field: ALL   Operator OR

Search Term: Field: ALL

Submit Query   Clear Query

Logout | Please logout when you are done to release system resources allocated for you.

TESS HOME | NEW USER | FREE FORM | BROWSE DICT | SEARCH OG | TOP | HELP

Figure 6-4 | "Structured Form Search" page

In the Structured Form search, type "nike" in the first box labeled "Search Term." To the right, in the box labeled "Field," select "Full Mark" from the list of possible fields on the drop-down menu. "Full Mark" is used because the word "nike" by itself is the complete trademark without any graphics or special symbols. This type of mark is called a "typed drawing" by the PTO. In the second "Search Term" box enter 025, and in the "Field" box to its right select "International Class." *Important:* before clicking the "Submit Query" button, make sure in the box to the far right that is identified as "Operator" that the Boolean term being used is "AND." The box defaults to "OR," and if it is not reset to "AND" the results will be confusing. The resulting page is shown in figure 6-5.

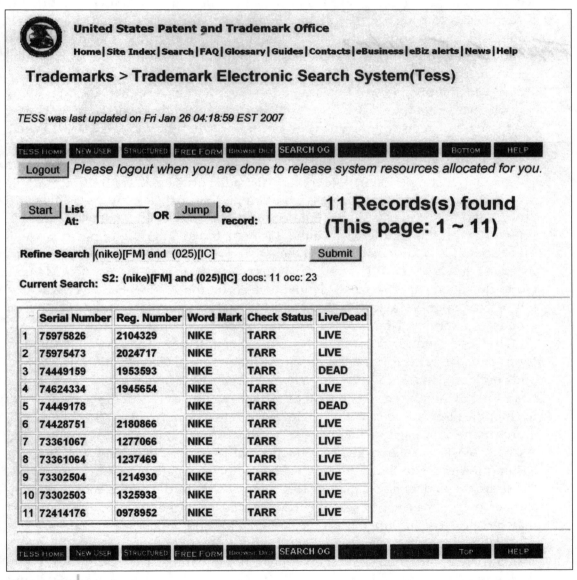

Figure 6-5

Results of a Structured Form search

There are eleven results shown. Since the searcher is looking for the first example of a typed drawing with the word "nike," select item 11 at the bottom, which will have the lowest serial number and be the oldest example of the typed drawing. This is the first trademark for the word "nike" used in connection with shoes and is dated January 31, 1972, and was located with a simple word search.

Searching Designs and Symbols

The search for a simple word is not a typical search. It was chosen because the techniques used will serve a searcher through other types of searches. Normally a searcher is looking for a word or phrase that is a possible trademark, not a trademark that is known to exist. The next trademark search is going to seek a symbol. The symbol being searched is the graphic symbol for Nike Corporation shown in figure 6-6.

Figure 6-6
The Nike "swoosh"

For the purposes of this search, assume that the searcher does not know whether or not the mark is registered, does not know the owner, does not know the date of registration, and does not know what the mark is called. Where should a searcher begin?

Earlier in this chapter, in the "Overview of the Search Process," there is a standard listing of the steps involved in a trademark search. For the first example search, the first steps of this process were skipped, since the example was the word "nike," and this term was simply entered to get a classification. That technique will not work with this example, since there is no name to enter. Entering "nike" will give thousands of false hits, so a searcher should try to search by the standard steps listed in the "Overview." The first step is to consult the Goods and Services Manual. Go to the Goods and Services Manual located on the PTO website, **www.uspto. gov > Trademarks > Other Guides and Manuals > Acceptable Identification of Goods and Services Manual.** The resulting page is shown in figure 6-7.

The Goods and Services Manual is an alphabetic listing of all allowable *keywords* for trademarks. This is not the same as the International Classification. The Goods and Services Manual is a keyword listing of terms appearing in the IC. If a searcher has no idea where a particular good or service would be classified, she comes here to enter the term and see what possible classifications it may appear in. For a novice searcher the first page of the manual, as shown in figure 6-7, is overwhelming. As with most instruction given in intellectual property books and websites, the assumption is made that a person already knows something about trademarks. There are seven data fields, and what is contained in the data fields means nothing to a person who has not yet seen the fields. At the top of the page are two items that may be selected. They are marked "Choose Field" and "Enter Search Terms."

On this page a searcher may enter a term or several terms, linked with AND, OR, and NOT, and then see if they appear in the manual. The first problem is to decide what term should be entered: "nike," "shoes," "athletic equipment," and "sports" all come to mind, but none identify the symbol shown. What word would

United States Patent and Trademark Office

Home | Site Index | Search | FAQ | Glossary | Guides | Contacts | eBusiness | eBiz alerts | News | Help

Trademarks > **Trademark Acceptable Identification of Goods & Services**

Help | Notices | Browse Entire Content | To suggest additions to the Trademark ID Manual click here

---

Search Manual

Choose Field | All fields | | **Enter Search Terms** | [_____]

[Submit Query] [Reset]

Trademark ID Manual Field Codes

Code & Name	Examples
[IC] Class Code	Ex: "001"[IC]
[GS] Goods or Services (G/S)	Ex: G[GS]
[ED] Effective Date	Ex: "20010601"[ED]
[DE] Descriptions	Ex: computer[DE]
[ST] Status (A, M, D)	Ex: A[ST]
[NT] Note	Ex: deleted[NT]
[TL] Trilateral	Ex: T[TL]

Click for list of **All Notes**

Quick Tips:

- *How to enter a search:*
  Enter search term(s) in search box. Use the Search list box to select the search field. The default "All Fields" will search all available fields (IC, GS, ED, DE and ST). Press "Submit Query" to execute the search. The "Reset" button will delete contents of the search box and will return to the "All Fields" selection.
- *Refine Search:*
  Use the Refine Search box located at the top of the results page to add terms to the original search. This search box may be used to execute new searches. To execute a new search, delete the contents of the search box, enter new text for searching and press "Submit Query" to execute the new search. The search will default to "All Fields". For specific fields, enter proper field code following the term.
- *Boolean Search Operators:*
  - AND (e.g., automobile and repair; "016" and paint)
    The search results will include only identifications containing both terms.
  - OR (e.g., cloth or fabric)
    The search results will include identifications containing either term, as well as

Figure 6-7

"Goods and Services Manual" page

identify the symbol? Popularly, the symbol is called a "swoosh," but when searching for trademarks, that knowledge is useless. The standard technique is to enter and search as many terms and their related terms and synonyms as possible.

Try shoes. Enter "shoes" in the "Search Terms" box shown in figure 6-7. The results appear all over the IC; however, "Athletic shoes" is listed and appears in IC 025. The reason this step is taken is to verify that the term being searched actually exists. It is like looking in the index to the yellow pages of the phone book to see under which heading a particular good or service is listed. Now what?

The second step in the standard procedure is to go to the IC and scan the listing to verify that IC 025 is the correct place. IC 025 is for "Clothing, footwear, headgear," which is not very detailed but seems to be the right IC. It is likely that this IC is where the swoosh will be located, since the swoosh appears on athletic shoes. Also helpful was the simple word search performed earlier in this chapter that showed the word "nike" appeared in IC 025.

The next step in the standard procedure is to go to the Trademark Manual of Examining Procedure and look in chapter 1400 of that manual for scope notes on IC 25. The TMEP is located at **www.uspto.gov > Trademarks > Other Guides and Manuals > Trademark Manual of Examining Procedure.**

Once there, click on "1400" under the "Chapters" section and scroll down to class 25 (unlike the IC that uses initial 0s, in the TMEP the initial 0 is deleted) in the resulting document. The TMEP says that included in class 25 are "Clothing, footwear, headgear," which is the exact wording of the IC, but it also includes an explanatory note saying that class 25 does not include certain clothing and footwear for special use and suggests that the searcher consult the alphabetical list of goods. This means that for rock-climbing shoes, for example, the trademark may appear in another IC. So is an athletic shoe special-use footwear? Go to the page shown in figure 6-7 and enter "athletic shoes" in the "Choose Field" box. The result shows that athletic shoes are classed in IC 025. So IC 025 is the right place. The searcher should ask herself, as a check, whether IC 025 is a class for a good or a service. After IC 034, all classes are for services and not goods. Is the swoosh being searched on a good or a service? If it is a service, IC 025 cannot be correct, but in this case the mark being searched appears on a good and not a service.

What ways are there to search a trademark that is a symbol? In figure 6-1 the third search option was for a Free Form search. The Free Form search is a way of searching any or all of fifty-one different fields within a trademark. Look at those fifty-one fields again by going to **www.uspto.gov > Trademarks > Search Trademarks** and clicking on "Free Form Search." The page is shown in figure 6-8.

At this point the searcher, assuming she has no other knowledge of this symbol, has only one piece of information: that the design appears on athletic shoes. A Free Form search, or any other trademark search, without at least one other piece of information is useless.

The next piece of information will be the design code under which this swoosh would be classified. The design code is a verbal explanation of what the symbol looks like. This is the only possible other piece of information that can be obtained in this situation.

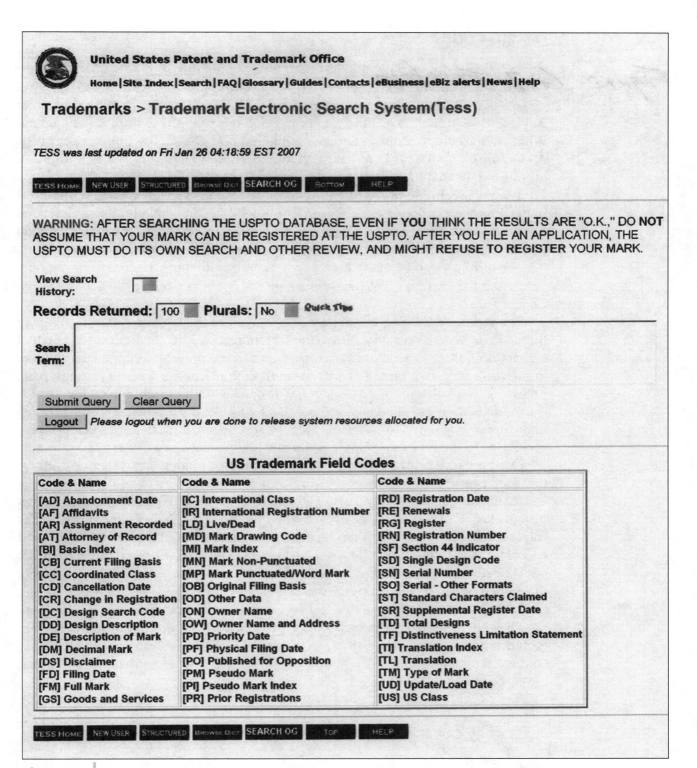

Figure 6-8

"Free Form Search" page

Design Codes

Go to the Design Search Code Manual, **www.uspto.gov > Trademarks > Other Guides and Manuals > Design Search Code Manual.** Before scanning the twenty-nine design code classes in this manual, try and describe what the swoosh symbol is. What does it look like? Plant or animal? Does it resemble a number or a letter? What are the components that make up this symbol? Does it resemble a deer horn? A chevron? A smile? A bent bar? A hook? A check mark? The key is to think of other symbols that look similar to this one.

To make scanning of the categories easier, if using Windows, go to **Edit > Find in Page** and enter "hook," or "chevron," or "check," or any other term that describes the symbol in question. Sometimes a lucky searcher will find the right design code by this method. The only other method is to scan the design codes.

The term "chevron" appears in design search code category 26. This is the only term from the searchers list that appears in the design code list. Click on "Design Category 26."

The top of the "Design Category 26" page gives the various types of things in this category, and by scrolling down the searcher can see that in addition to a textual explanation, there is a graphic representation of the types of symbols that appear in each category. If not familiar with the terminology for the types of symbols (e.g., polygons, quadrilaterals), the easiest way for an amateur searcher to review the list is to scan it and try to pick out a symbol that looks like the one being searched. Each major area of category 26 has a subcategory and further subcategories that get very specific as to the type of design that fits into a given category.

Design class 24.17.12, identified as "Chevrons and angles," shows three symbols that look pretty close to a swoosh. Eureka!

In practice, a searcher would not stop here even though it seems that the proper design class has been located. A searcher would go through this same process with each term she could think of as describing the swoosh until she was sure that she had at least one, and hopefully several, proper design classes, since trademarks are not classed in only one design class. For this particular example, while check marks did not show up in the listing of the 29 design codes, check marks are in design class 24.17.15, showing three designs very similar to the swoosh. (See figure 6-9.)

These designs would have been located only with a more thorough check of each design category, especially since these designs are in a category described as "Notational signs and symbols" in a category listed as "Heraldry, flags, crowns, crosses, arrows and symbols."

Figure 6-9 | Check mark symbols found in search of design code categories

Back to the Free Form Search

The Free Form search shown in figure 6-8 allows the searcher to combine terms and data elements that may appear in specific fields within a trademark document. Before searching for design codes the searcher had only one piece of data, the IC 025. Now, with a possible design code, the searcher should be able to join these two pieces of information to locate a trademark that appears similar to the swoosh being searched. Although with just two pieces of information a design trademark can be located, the resulting list of hits is still quite long sometimes. In the swoosh example, entering the two pieces of information—the IC and the design code— would yield over 1,000 hits. With one more piece of information that list could be greatly diminished. For example, by adding "footwear" to the search as a description of the good or service, a term that was used to describe IC 025, the list can be shortened to about 300 hits. (See figure 6-7 above.)

There are fifty-one categories of things to search in the Free Form search, and any piece of information that fits one of the fifty-one fields of search can be added to shorten the list—if the searcher is able to provide one more piece of information. In the swoosh example, if the searcher had the knowledge that the mark being searched was owned by Nike Corporation, the search is simple.

In the "Search Term" box in figure 6-8, the searcher would enter the information for the IC, the design code, and the trademark owner in this fashion:

025[ic] AND 261712[dc] AND nike[on]

The resulting list is shown in figure 6-10. If the first item on the list is selected, the trademark that results is shown in figure 6-11. The search has found the Nike swoosh symbol.

Getting Assistance with Trademarks

Many similar or exact matches of words appear in registered trademarks. A listing of some of these was shown in the beginning of this chapter. The determining factor in how similar two marks may be, even if they appear in different ICs, is whether the similar marks will cause confusion in the mind of the consumer. That decision can be made by a patent and trademark attorney or, in many cases, by the courts.

In a search for a word, the important principle is to eliminate those words that are definitely unlike the term being searched and to keep records of those about which the searcher is doubtful. If an attorney is hired to complete a search or to make an application for a person wishing to trademark a word, having records of what has been searched and found will eliminate the need for the attorney to duplicate the work that has already been done. In situations like these, when a searcher is unsure as to whether to proceed with a search due to restrictions, the best thing to do is to seek legal counsel. The time and money spent searching and registering a trademark can amount to much more than that spent on employing competent counsel.

United States Patent and Trademark Office

Home | Site Index | Search | FAQ | Glossary | Guides | Contacts | eBusiness | eBiz alerts | News | Help

Trademarks > Trademark Electronic Search System(Tess)

TESS was last updated on Fri Jan 26 04:18:59 EST 2007

| TESS HOME | NEW USER | STRUCTURED | FREE FORM | BROWSE DICT | SEARCH OG | PREV LIST | NEXT LIST | BOTTOM | HELP |

Logout | *Please logout when you are done to release system resources allocated for you.*

Start | List At: [   ] OR Jump to record: [   ] — **15 Records(s) found (This page: 1 ~ 15)**

Refine Search [025[ic] and 261712[dc] and nike[on]]   Submit

Current Search: S1: 025[ic] and 261712[dc] and nike[on] docs: 15 occ: 47

	Serial Number	Reg. Number	Word Mark	Check Status	Live/Dead
1	75975826	2104329	NIKE	TARR	LIVE
2	75975473	2024717	NIKE	TARR	LIVE
3	75034391		TC TOTAL CONDITIONING	TARR	DEAD
4	75034390	2164358	ACG	TARR	LIVE
5	74802828	2056812		TARR	LIVE
6	74802703	2009982	SPORTS SPECIALTIES	TARR	LIVE
7	74801284	1798795	NIKE PREMIER	TARR	DEAD
8	74428751	2180866	NIKE	TARR	LIVE
9	74133429		NIKE PREMIER	TARR	DEAD
10	73093928	1086959		TARR	DEAD
11	73368773	1284386	NIKE AIR	TARR	LIVE
12	73361065	1284385		TARR	LIVE
13	73302507	1323342		TARR	LIVE
14	73302503	1325938	NIKE	TARR	LIVE
15	72414177	0977190		TARR	LIVE

| TESS HOME | NEW USER | STRUCTURED | FREE FORM | BROWSE DICT | SEARCH OG | PREV LIST | NEXT LIST | TOP | HELP |

Figure 6-10 | Results of a Free Form search using class, design code, and term

United States Patent and Trademark Office

Home | Site Index | Search | FAQ | Glossary | Guides | Contacts | eBusiness | eBiz alerts | News | Help

Trademarks > Trademark Electronic Search System(Tess)

TESS was last updated on Fri Jan 26 04:18:59 EST 2007

| TESS HOME | NEW USER | STRUCTURED | FREE FORM | BROWSE DICT | SEARCH OG | BOTTOM | HELP | PREV LIST | CURR LIST |
| NEXT LIST | FIRST DOC | PREV DOC | NEXT DOC | LAST DOC |

Logout | Please logout when you are done to release system resources allocated for you.

Start | List At: [   ] OR Jump | to record: [   ] **Record 1 out of 15**

| TARR Status | ASSIGN Status | TDR | TTAB Status | *(Use the "Back" button òf the Internet Browser to return to TESS)*

Word Mark	NIKE
Goods and Services	IC 025. US 022 039. G & S: footwear. FIRST USE: 19960713. FIRST USE IN COMMERCE: 19960713
Mark Drawing Code	(3) DESIGN PLUS WORDS, LETTERS, AND/OR NUMBERS
Design Search Code	26.17.12 - Angles (geometric); Chevrons
Serial Number	75975826
Filing Date	August 26, 1993
Current Filing Basis	1A
Original Filing Basis	1B
Published for Opposition	February 28, 1995
Registration Number	2104329
Registration Date	October 7, 1997
Owner	(REGISTRANT) BRS, Inc. CORPORATION OREGON One Bowerman Drive Beaverton OREGON 97005
	(LAST LISTED OWNER) NIKE, INC. CORPORATION OREGON ONE BOWERMAN DRIVE BEAVERTON OREGON 970056453

Figure 6-11

The Nike swoosh trademark

There are also many private services that will perform a trademark search for you. Fees for this service and what the service includes vary greatly. Check the Internet under "trademark searching service" to locate hundreds of these services.

Trademarks may be in use but not registered at the state or federal level. In this case, a search engine such as Google can be used to search the term for possible matches anywhere on the Internet.

Intellectual Property Codes in Verse

I n August 2006 *American Libraries* magazine published a short blurb in the magazine's By the Numbers section stating that Yehuda Berlinger, who produces a blog on gaming at http://jergames.blogspot.com, had posted a version of the Copyright Code of the United States in a poem that ran 136 sections. I read the code in verse and at first thought that it was nothing more than clever and whimsical.

I work with the Copyright Code, Title 17 of the U.S. Code, frequently and often have a difficult time locating a particular section of the code because it does not have an index—it has only brief phrases describing each chapter. Berlinger's poem became very useful to me, since it describes every section of the code in plain English and works beautifully in locating parts of the code.

When I contacted Yehuda to thank him and tell him how useful his "Copyright Code in Verse" was to me, he volunteered to write the trademark and patent codes in verse too if they would be of use. I am including all three IP codes in verse here in the hopes that they will be valuable to those who work with intellectual property law.

The U.S. Copyright Code in Verse

These verses describe
All the copyright code
Of the U. S. of A.
Written down as an ode

Some detail is lost
As you might have expected
A brief note about some
Of what was rejected

For most of the things
That you aren't to do
There's always exceptions
In one case or two

Most often a teacher
Can break all these rules
In order to teach in
A setting like school

And also a scientist
Or engineer, too,
Has leeway to copy
An item or two

There are other exceptions:
Recording for blind ones
Or making performance
For blind or for veterans

But I'm not a lawyer
Don't rely just on me
Go find one to ask,
Better yet, two or three

1

101
We start off defining
People and media
Terms you can also find
On Wikipedia

102
Copyright is for writings,
Music, dance, drama,
Movies, buildings everywhere
Even Alabama

103
Copyright applies even
When you're deriving
From copyrighted works
And no, I ain't jiving

104
Copyright applies to works
From any countries
Assuming they're smart
  enough
To sign the right treaties

104A
If copyright is restored
All others must cease
If the owner gives notice
For twelve months, at least

105
Nothing the government
Makes is copyrighted
But they can buy copyrights
At K-Mart sales, red-lighted

106
The owner exclusively
Can perform or display,
Copy, derive, or market
But do not dismay (see 107)

106A
Visual arts owners only
Can claim attribution
Or prevent any display
On threat of retribution

107
Despite all of these rights
All people can reproduce
To report, criticize, or teach
Because that is fair use

108
And libraries, too, can make
Copies for archiving
If the works are all public
And no money deriving

109
You can always sell off
What you've legally bought,
  honey
But you can't lease or rent it
If you're doing it for money

110
Teachers, priests, and vendors
Can perform without charge
And also for blind people
Or veterans, small or large

111
Rebroadcasting without changes
To hotel guests is fine
If not saved, not commercialized
And sent at the same time

112
You can even make copies
To rebroadcast later
If you then take these copies
And put them through a grater

113
If your graphical work
Is on something useful
It's copyable; you'd better
Go back to art school

114
Sound recordings, but not
  music
Can be re-performed
As long as it's attributed
And not grossly malformed

115
Non-dramatic music
Whatever that means
Can be forcibly licensed
On a per-copy scheme

116
The same situation
Applies to jukeboxes
Without further "withal"s
"provisions" or "ad-hoc"ses

117
Copies of software
Can be made as a backup
Or copied to memory
In prepping for setup

118
Owners of copyrights
Can license them out;
For non-dramatic work
That's all it's about

119
You can also rebroadcast
To boost your own signal
But altering or storing
Is a violation, willful

120
Architectural copyright
Includes only the object
You can photograph or draw it
Or break it without respect

121
Non-dramatic writing
Can be copied for the blind
As a phonographic work
And that's even if you mind

122
Generally speaking
You can retransmit signals
Altering or commercializing
  them
Is mucho violation, willful

2

201

You own what you made
Unless working for hire
In a group, only your part
But you'll be much less tired

202

Owning work doesn't mean
Owning the container;
And you own the container
Not the work; could I be
    plainer?

203

If the copyright owner
Should sound the deathly
    chime
The spouse and kids gain
    ownership
For a heck of a long time

204

Copyright ownership
Is transferred in writing
And not by pinkie fingers
Or elephant biting

205

You can register transfers
With the office of copyrighting
But first come first served
No pushing no fighting

3

301

As far as I can tell
And I'm no expert yet
This section talks only about
What sections come next?

302

A copyright lasts seventy years
After you're dead
Or ninety years generally
If they can't find your head

303

If written before '78
But published only since
Go back to the last section
And try not to wince

304

If written before '78
Your copyright's expired
But Sonny Bono changed that
Before he retired

305

All rights to a copyright
End when the year does
By which we mean calendar
    year
Eight days after Santa Claus

4

401

You can copyright notice
But you really don't have to
Put circle-C or "Copyright"
The name and the year, too

402

Sound recordings use circle-P
Which I never knew
And frankly I must say
I've never seen one, too

403

If mostly governmental
No copyright is needed
But a mixture may warrant one
So that notice is heeded

404

One copyright notice
Is sufficient for collections
Each author can place one
So he won't feel rejection

405

Before Berne's convention
And without copyright notice
Infringement was as innocent
As a butterfly on a lotus

406

Similarly, before Berne,
If the notice was erroneous
An infringer could claim
    innocence
Of all acts felonious

407

If you register your copyright
Don't loosen your collar
You're no more protected
And you're out thirty dollars

408

You don't have to send
The whole work in a truck
Just send the first part of it
With a check for thirty bucks

409

Just fill out the form
Fill in all of the blanks
And don't forget the money
The next trip to the bank

410

For registering, you'll get
A nice form in the mail
A judge may take notice of it
And throw someone in jail

411

You may need to register
To sue for infringing
Proving violation
Is on what this is hinging

412

In some cases damages
Can only be collected
After registered copyright
Has been properly inspected

5

501

If you violate copyright
You're a copyright infringer
Not a pirate, nor a robber,
Nor an alcohol binger

502

Any valid courthouse
Anywhere in the states
Can examine the infringement
And determine its fate

503

The court can decide to
Impound all the copies
And have them destroyed
Whether tapes, books, or
　　floppies

504

You may become liable for
Both profits and damages
Not more than 150K
Paid in dollars, not sandwiches

505

You may also have to pay
For the lawyerly costs
A fee known to make tremble
Even heavenly hosts

506

If you willfully copied
Or sold things for moolah
Or fraudulently copyrighted
You're a criminal, so woo hah

507

You can't be a criminal
If five years have passed
And no civil actions
If three years have amassed

508

Certain types of letters
Will be passed here and there
One month after filing
So pull up a chair

509

If they find copying hardware
("Now you're cold . . . ooh,
　　you're getting warmer!")
They may take it and pay off
Agent fees and informers

510

Any infringers
Of the cable persuasion
May lose, for thirty days
Their license, on occasion

511

Governmental employees
Will be dealt with as hard
So has anybody checked yet
On the president's iPod?

512

ISPs, unless notified,
Even if they take action
Are not liable if you store on
　　them
Illegal songs from Michael
　　Jackson

513

If you charge way too much
For your performance rights
The public can sue and get
Relief from this plight

6

601

You can't bring to the U.S.
Any written stuff
Unless published here or
　　Canada
Amazingly enough

602

The same goes for
　　phonorecords
And copies illegal
So no photocopies
Of Charles Schulz's beagle

603

You can apply to bring these in
But they probably won't let you
If you try to bring them
　　anyway
Custom agents will get you

7

701

The Copyright Office
Is staffed by some smarties
They advise and they poll
And throw pretty good parties

702

They also make laws
Like the ones that you're
　　reading
To change just one sentence
Takes 'bout five hundred
　　meetings

703

Any dates that are mentioned
Fall on next business day
I must say it's clearer
When written this way

704

The stuff that you send them
To register claims
May get filed or made
Into paper airplanes

705

They file, they stamp
And they make a big list
And they try to make sure
That no papers get missed

706

In a strange sense of irony
Befitting this bill
The Copyright Office
Can copy anything at will

707

They publish a record
Of all copyrights made
And they'll hand out
    applications
And then send you away

708

They sure seem to charge you
For all sorts of things
After leaving the office
Check your jewelry and rings

709

If your mail gets delayed
They may give you a break
Otherwise it'd interfere with
The money they'd take

8

801

A royalty panel
May certain problems fix
I thought we abandoned
    royalty
In 1776

802

A royalty panel
Is like a secret boys' club
To get in you have to know
The secret hand rub

803

Any owner affected
By new royalty rates
Can argue about them
If they're feeling irate

9

901

This section is all about
Semiconductors
There's no rhyme for this word
So la la la luctor

902

Actually it deals with
Circuit mask creation
But only for nationals
And original work done

903

Mask copyrights are like others
Upon closer inspection
So frankly I don't see
The point of this section

904

Mask copyright lasts
For only ten years
The same length to which all
Other ones should be sheared

905

Only the mask owner
Can use the mask, duh.
I can't believe this chapter
Is fourteen sections, no suh

906

Here's something: a mask
    may be
Reverse engineered
Just not copied directly
Now, isn't that queer?

907

Only the infringer
Is liable and wrong
If you bought a copied chip
You can move right along

908

You can register a mask work
Within two years it's made
And then it is recognized
Only—surprise!—if you've
    paid

909

A notice on a mask work
Is a circle 'round an "M"
Once again, I say I've
Never seen one of them

910

If you copy a mask work
Without the permission
The government will use your
    head
For research on fission

911

Damages for mask copying
You will have to pay
Your equipment and profits
And maybe 250K

912

The laws in this chapter
Preempt laws of states
But other federal laws
Might make these dissipate

913

Your liability here
Might depend on the date
Be sure to read this section
Before you violate

914

These laws apply not just here
But in all member states
We will try to stop violations
Unless we're too late

10

1001

This section defines
Many audio words
Audio is stuff that's
Not seen, but is heard

1002

All audio devices
Must have copy controls
The reasons for this
The RIAA extols

1003
Even with copy con-
Trols, you must pay
A "just-in-case" fee
To the RIAA

1004
One dollar at least
For each audio device
But it may be that twelve
Is as high as the price

1005
The Treasury holds on to
All of this money
And makes interest on it, too,
Now isn't that funny?

1006
If someone makes claims
That their work has been taped
They might get some money
From the Treasury's take

1007
They can file and make claims
And all sorts of disputes
In the end it comes down to
Those guys in the suits

1008
The devices themselves
Are not covered herein
And neither is illegal
Song copyin'

1009
If you didn't include any
Copy controls
You may have to pay
'Bout a thousand Royce Rolls

1010
To sue someone for
Their sub-standard devices
Lots of letters go back and
       forth
Once, twice, and thrices

11

1101
This little chapter
Only says that it's wrong
To surreptitiously
Tape someone's song

12

1201
You cannot reverse
Any copy hardware
Nor sell any products
That do so, beware
Nor make VCRs
Without them, don't dare

1202
Don't mess with the notice
Of copyright law
Or remove it, or people
Will say they "never saw"

1203
If damaged by one of
The previous things
Take them to court
Until one of them sings

1204
If willfully done
You will pay a high price
And double the bill
If you do the thing twice

1205
A funny little clause here
It sure seems to me
It says that these sections
Don't trump privacy

13

1301
This chapter deals mostly
With vessels and hulls
I hope I can write it
Without being dull

1302
Designs must be new
And of uncommon shape
They can't look like something
A child could make

1303
When working on something
Already in place
A new thing's created
If it has a new face

1304
The design is protected
Only after it's shown
Or to the appropriate
Registers known

1305
The design is protected
For only a decade
And then any person
Can use what you've made

1306
The sign of a copyrighted
Design is a letter
A "D" in a circle—
The mask one is better

1307
Without the "D" notice
You can't collect costs
In fact, if someone started
You must pay what he lost

1308
Only the designer
Can make objects galore
Although, frankly, I thought
That's what patents are for

1309
As usual, if you make
An object protected
You've infringed, although
       exceptions
Are not here neglected

1310
You've only got two years
To claim your design
So hurry and don't forget
To pay up in time

1311
But if you have already
Filed the design
In some other country
It'll all turn out fine

1312
When swearing an oath
You can do it in writing
I'm not talking here
About swearing while fighting

1313
Your filed design
Is examined by those
Who may say it's good or
May not; well, who knows?

1314
If you get a certificate
The design will be mentioned
Its shape and its form
And all its intention

1315
The office will publish
A list of inventions
In order to forgo
Invention contention

1316
And here's no surprise
To register costs dough
You should know, and that's
    why
I'm telling you so

1317
More rules may be added
As they go along
This verse is much longer
Than the section is long

1318
You can always obtain
A copy of your stuff
As if 1315
Just wasn't enough

1319
If any mistakes
On the records are found
They might get corrected
If someone's around

1320
Your rights can be transferred
If you're so inclined
And also the recipient
Doesn't really mind

1321
Any infringers must
Correct their ways
If given some notice
At least sixty days

1322
A judge may then order
An injunction of sorts
And the case may be taken
And decided by courts

1323
A fine for misdeeds
Is a 50K min
And all of your profits
From doing your sin

1324
Sometimes, however
The court may decide
The entire proceedings
Should be cast aside

1325
For falsely declaring
That someone must pay
You'll be rapped on the
    knuckles
And fined 'bout 10K

1326
For falsely inscribing
A design copyright
It's 500 bucks
And you won't sleep at night

1327
Any other actions
Of lying 'bout this
Will lose you some money
Which surely you'll miss

1328
For some reason here
It's the USPS
That must get involved
Into this sort of mess

1329
Ah, here we go now, this
Says patents applied
Will throw any design copy-
Rights to the side

1330
Design rules are subject
To trademark law, too
So don't misapply them
You'll pay if you do

1331
In all that was said here
The Copyright Office
Means Library of Congress
To be quite precise

1332
They're not retroactive
These laws written here
They only apply to things
After this year

Except for a preface
And appendices few
That's it, do enjoy and
Have a good day, too.

The U.S. Trademark Code in Verse

This verse is just some
Of United States Code
Fifteen, part twenty-two,
Written down as an ode

This part only deals
With the laws of trademark
I write them in poetry
To be less in the dark

It's not 'cause I'm bored
Or I want to be nice
My transcribing works as
A mnemonic device

You see, I read laws
And I put them to verse
And it helps me remember
For better or worse

My summaries are simplified
As you might well expect
Relying on my poetry would
Be most incorrect

Go read the original
If you want to know more
And have your whole legal
Protection assured

(By the way, if you've time
The rest of fifteen
Is a wild bunch of laws
It's really quite keen)

1051

If you own a mark that's
Really used in commerce
Pay heed to the directions
Written down in this verse

You must "own" the
    trademark
(Though it doesn't say how)
And you must promise to use it
Or be using it now

1052

The mark may be neither
Immoral nor deceptive
It must be unique and
Not simply descriptive

1053

Service marks are marks, too
But you need not be nervous
They only imply branding
They don't imply service

1054

And then there are other
    marks—
Like certification—
That serve to mark only
An organization

1055

This section lets you license
Your mark to some company
And let's you control it
Both branding and quality

1056

When registering marks
You may have to forgo
Some part of it, if the
Director says so

1057

You fill out the forms
In duplicate and triplicate
And then you receive
A nice legal certificate

1058

It's good for ten years
Or it's good for six, maybe
Either way, pay the fees
Or goodbye to your baby

1059

An identifying trademark's
Life can be extended
Although after ten years, it
Should probably be ended

1060

Trademarks can be transferred
If it's all done in writing
It's nice when done pleasantly
Without any fighting

1061

If some swearing is needed
To affirm an acknowledgment
My kids can teach you; they
Practice swearing they're
    innocent

1062

Just when your rights are
Secured, it gets better—
Your marks are all published
In many newsletters

1063

If you object to a trademark
As many people do
The office is happy to
Take your money, too

1064

A worker may cancel it
If he's had a bad day
A hangover, for instance,
Or his spouse is away

1065

But if no one objects
In the space of five years
Your trademark's assured
You can break out the beers

1066

If they made a mistake
And your mark's not unique
The Director may apologize
In a manner most meek

1067

In all of these cases
When people have problems
An appeal board gets formed
In order to solve them

1068
In the end, the Director
Simply does what he feels
So invite him to dinner
And cook a nice meal

1069
This section may be short but
Here's what the catch is:
It uses some strange words like
"Estoppel" and "laches"

1070
You pay registration and
You pay if you fight
So the fact that you pay to
Appeal seems 'bout right

1071
The Federal Circuit then
Handles the appeal
And then the fed judges
Can do what they feel

1072
Remember I said you register
Only if you "own" the mark?
Well ownership is established
By registering; that's a lark

1091
A supplemental register
May also exist
You don't register supplements
(I checked up on this)

1092
It's a different book for
trademarks
And it's pretty amusing
It's published, but it isn't,
which
Can get quite confusing

1093
The certificate for these types of
Listings is different
It's painted on noodles
With twenty-two pigments

1094
Apparently, these trademarks
are
Mostly like real ones
They follow the same rules
With minor exceptions

1095
These marks aren't unique
enough
For all practicality
If they are, you can upgrade
them to
Full-fledged legality

1096
These marks don't stop
imports
But to be quite concise,
I don't get this chapter and
I've read through it twice

1111
To mark something's
registered
Put an "R" in a ring
If you fail to, and then sue,
You won't get a thing

1112
The Director establishes a
Classification
In which to file all types
Of mark registration

1113
They charge you for
everything
Bring money in jerry-cans
You're only exempt if you're
Native American

1114
You're told you must stop for
Innocent violation
Whether using it in print
Or domain registration

1115
Numerous defenses against
Infringement are granted
None of those listed cover
"Because I wanted"

1116
The court then make noises
It shuffles and snorts
And it tries to make sense
Of a case of this sort

1117
The damages you might
pay are
Exceedingly high
You can kiss that new Rolls
Royce
You wanted goodbye

1118
You may then be forced to
Destroy every item
They'll soak them in gasoline
And then they will light 'em

1119
But the court may correct, if
It feels there's an error,
Any trademark mistakes in the
Trademark book ledger

1120
If you fraudulently trade-
marked
You naughty girl or boy
You're subject to lawsuits from
Those you've annoyed

1121
The states can make judgments
On cases like this
But they can't force new
markings
Or get them dismissed

1122
Federal and state workers
In all types of governments
Are subject to these laws
Regardless of consequence

1123
As usual, the Director can
Make up more laws
Whenever he wants to,
No "if"s or "because"

1124
You can't import goods
    bearing
Trademark violations
They have to stay inside
Their origin nations

1125
Don't misrepresent any
Product or service
Or pretend that you're
    famous—
Famous people get nervous

1126
We register trademarks from
All types of nations
But only from those with which
We have relations

1127
For some reason, definitions
Are only placed here
Instead of the beginning
Which would be more clear

1128
A fancy falutin'
Council must be formed
To discuss IP issues
And stay well informed

1129
Don't use famous people for
Your Internet domain
They've more money than you
And they're often insane

1141
This chapter says we work with
Other nations, too
And pretty much doesn't say
Anything else new

1141a
You can register trademarks
In more than one nation
And you only need fill out
A single application

1141b
When checking your claim
The Director is thorough
If it's good, it goes on to
The international bureau

1141c
If a trademark's abandoned,
Cancelled, or expired,
The bureau is notified if
The Director's not tired

1141d
Requests for extensions
Can be made here or there
As long as you've paid up
They really don't care

1141e
Extensions are based on the
Laws of this section
Other laws you may read
May just be misdirection

1141f
This whole chapter simply
Just says what we do:
We do whatever international
Court tells us to

1141g
Really, it just goes on
About dates and priority
A pretty dull subject within
Intellectual Property

1141h
When refusing a local mark
We don't have to be nice
When dealing with foreign
    ones
We tend to think twice

1141i
We'll send the certificates
Any place you're alive
Even to "Under the stairs,
Nine Privet Drive"

1141j
Oh brother, some more boring
Rules are now made
Whomever wrote this section
Was grossly overpaid

1141k
An affidavit is needed
To prove any marking
Is really being used,
You're not allowed Free
    Parking

1141l
We only will deal with
A person from nations
Who like us and say so—
We need affirmation

1141m
Your five years of usage
Begins with your signing
After which it's incontestable
No tantrums, no whining

1141n
Any rights to a trademark
Continue with extensions
You should register with the
    same name
To avoid all contention

There are other subsections
That may also apply
But this is all the current
Section supplies

The others are references
And simply point here
So I'll just say good night, and
Have sweet dreams, my dear

The U.S. Patent Code in Verse

These verses are part
Thirty-five of the code
Of the U. S. of A.
Written down as an ode

They summarize patent law
Most generally
But don't cover every fine
Detail, you see

For instance small business
Pays half the fees stated
This info was left out
Of what was related

So what I have written
Be it naughty or nice
Is no substitute for real
Legal advice

(And where I write "he"
I don't mean to insist
That a man is implied
I'm not that Chauvinist)

Part I

1
This section establishes
The office, PT
And says that it's located
In Washington, D.C.

2
The office can do what
It does, naturally
Make patents and trademarks
For people to see

3
There's directors, commis-
      sioners,
And lawyers there, too
They all should be trained
So they know what to do

4
Anyone working there
In any capacity
Can't claim any patents,
To ensure their veracity

5
The patent dispensers
Can't sit and look pretty
They have to take heed of
An advisory committee

6
After making decisions,
Either "yes" or "rejected,"
A board of appeals may now
Change what they just did

7
The Director can't only
Depend on his looks
He has to be smart and
Read plenty of books

8
The Director may also
Reclassify subjects
In order to help decide
Accepts or rejects

9
The Director may give—
He's got nothing to hide—
Copies of patents and
Pics, certified

10
He also may publish
This stuff in a journal
So it can be read by
All people, external

11
He can also give copies
To foreigners; although
Only if they're from NAFTA
Or the WTO

12
Libraries also
Get copies each year
They make for good doorstops
Or so I do hear

13
In June every year
He reports the amount
Of money left in the
PTO's bank account

21
If you pay any fees, you
Can now feel relieved—
The postmark establishes
When they're received

22
Documents received can be
Sent in by mail
Either electronic
Or delivered by snail

23
If you need to appear in
A court to testify
The Director may tell you
What rules will apply

24
If you are a witness
It's no cause to unravel
They pay for your trouble
And also your travel

25
Some things you can mail in
If signed, under oath
Lying may cost money,
Or imprisonment, or both

26
Documents may sometimes be
Accepted when wrong
If corrected ones will soon
Be following along

32
The Director can fire people
Pretty much when he feels
(If you're wondering,
    section 31
Has since been repealed)

33
Pretending to practice
In the patenting field
Will cost you a thousand bucks
When your guilt is revealed

41
There's all sorts of fees
To be paid for this service
If you're six months past due
You had better be nervous

42
The fees get collected
And used to pay costs
Important info without which
You'd surely be lost

Part II

100
Some words are defined here
To prevent all contention
For instance: "invention"
    means
Uh, well it means "invention"

101
Patents are for processes,
Machines, or compositions,
Or improvements thereof,
Subject to conditions

102
If already known
Or in print, or described,
Or abandoned, a patent
Cannot be applied

103
A process that anyone could
Discover's superfluous
You can't patent it, for it's
Patently obvious

104
You can only claim patent
If you made the invention
In a country with which we
Have no contention

105
If you come from outer space
The rules aren't dismissed
Apparently this applies to
The lawyers who wrote this

111
To apply for a patent
You fill out in writing
And you swear and you pay
Isn't that exciting?

112
You fill out your claim
About what the thing does
And how it all works
And wherefore and because

113
You can send in some pictures
To make your case clear
You can use finger paints
If your children are near

114
You may need to send in a
Working model, too
For things biological
You send in some goo

115
You then make an oath
That you're telling the truth
And then go to dinner
And drink your vermouth

116
Inventors join forces if
Co-invention is proved
You can also join later
Or have your name removed

117
If you're dead, your estate
Might on patents insist;
Wait, if you're dead, how
Are you reading this?

118
If you don't want to patent
Don't worry too much
Let someone else do it
For a fee or some such

119
If you're already registered
Outside the states
You are retroactively granted
Within a year of the date

120
A follow-up patent
Is often permitted
To be dated to when the
First one was submitted

121
Two inventions should not
Be submitted together
So split them, and next time
Don't try to be clever

122
Patent applications are
Kept in obscurity
Especially ones that
Affect national security

131
A mysterious section;
It says the Director
Will don trench coat and specs
And become an inspector

132

If rejected, a letter to
The inventor goes flying
It says, "Sorry. No good. But
Thank you for trying."

133

If you fail to reply
To a letter you get
Your application is invalid
Which you'll surely regret

134

If you twice get rejected
I know just how you feel
Take heart, and complain to
The Board of Appeals

135

Interference is when
Two patents disagree
Kind of like in football
Terminology

141

If you're still unhappy, you
Can complain higher up;
Has anyone else noticed that
The numbering is screwed up?

142

Just go to the Federal
Circuit to yell
Was that "Circuit" or
    "Circus"?
How can anyone tell?

143

The Circuit (or Circus)
Will request all the docs
And the PTO sends them
Overnight in a box

144

It decides what to do
And will tell you quite freely
You can bribe them with small
    bills
Or gifts (no, not really)

145

Weirder yet, if you don't like
Federals of that sort,
You can yell at the office
And take them to court

146

And the same thing applies
For interference probs,
But you probably won't win
If you break down in sobs

151

If your patent is granted
You'll get it the day
That you break out your wallet
And finally pay

152

An assignee can also
Receive it for you
Make sure he remembers
To pass it on, too

153

The patent is stamped, and
It's signed and it's sealed
And it's boiled and basted
And posted and peeled

154

The patent applies in the
Days and the nights
For the next twenty years
Giving exclusive rights

155

You can't extend patents
For even one day
Unless pending research
By the FDA

155A

An exception is made
To give extension
For drugs made during
    Carter's
Administration

156

More exceptions are granted
For DNA and stuff
To ensure that they have been
Tested enough

157

Statutory registration
May also be involved
Even before other
Issues are solved

161

A whole chapter follows
Devoted to plants
There's no such provision
For new types of ants

162

Why not? Ants are much
Cuter than greenery
They crawl upside down
And they brighten the scenery

163

And ants are important
They aerate the ground
And they clean up dead leaves
Wherever they're found

164

By the way, you may notice
That plants I'm ignoring
It's mostly because this
Whole chapter was boring

171

This next chapter talks about
Patents for design
Get out your finger paints
And step up to the line

172

The previous priority
System's used here
For checking the dates
Day and month, and the year

173
Design patents last only
For fourteen years
By which time the next fad
Of style appears

181
Some patents are secret
For national fears
This secrecy must be
Renewed every year

182
Any secret patent will
Be quickly removed
If filing in some other
Country is proved

183
If secrecy harms you
You'll be compensated
Important people tell you
How this is calculated

184
A regular patent you
Filed for here
Can be filed abroad if
You wait half a year

185
You can only do that
With a license obtained
Without it you'll lose
Unless error is claimed

186
Publishing secrets is
Really uncool
A lesson you should have
    learned
Back in high school

187
Permission is granted
To people who warrant
If you have to ask, then you
Certainly aren't

188
More rules can be written
About secrecy
And hidden in places
Where no one can see

200
This chapter deals mostly
With federally assisted
Inventions; yours wasn't
You probably missed it

201
More plain definitions are
Written out here
In order to make sure
All meanings are clear

202
Sometimes the government
Let's you keep what you made
It depends on a poker game
Who won, and who played

203
Even when the government
Doesn't make you lose it
They'll probably force you
To let them use it

204
If you license it out
In any circumstance
You must give U.S.
Companies first chance

205
The feds won't blab secrets
With their interests at stake
It might interfere
With the money they'd make

206
Once again, here's a clause
That if these rules are lacking
More rules may be created
With federal backing

207
Federal agencies
Should hold patents, because
They could patent up "war"
Before somebody else does

208
All parts of the government
Every hill, town, and alley
Must listen to the government
Except Tennessee Valley
    (it's true)

209
A federal patent
Can be licensed to mentors
Who may actually need it
Like "Bob's House of Inventors"

210
A really long section
That talks about precedence
And goes on for pages
With little or no consequence

211
These special regulations
For citizens governmental
Won't help you in the least
For any acts criminal

212
Educational grants are
Not covered by these
Laws; so go patent
Your blue college cheese

Part III

251
If a patent's defective
As some are, naturally,
You can have them updated
If you pay the right fee

252
The old one is replaced by
The new. Too bad we
Can't as simply replace a bad
Personality

253
A partial invalidation
Doesn't wreck the whole claim
Just mark what's in error and
Find someone to blame

254
If the office made an error
The Director must pontificate
Whether to correct it
Or issue a certificate

255
If the applicant made the error
The choices are the same
But corrections cost money
To stay in the game

256
You can even have names
Corrected within,
You should spell your name
     correctly
When you first send it in

261
Patents are property
According to this small part
You can sell them, or trade
     them,
Or buy them at Wal-Mart

262
Each owner in joint can
Sell his part or hers
Regardless of what the
Other owners prefer

267
If the patent is needed
By the U.S. armed forces
All dates are extended
As a matter of courses

271
Using patented methods
Or a patented device
Is considered infringement
And it isn't quite nice

272
But patented engines
Not available here
Can be used in your vehicle
Without any fear

273
New patents released cannot
Cause an infraction
A year after you started
Doing your action

281
The civil court rules
On all cases without fuss
Because patent infringement
Just isn't civil-rous

282
You can claim in defense
That the patent is wrong
Or the claims that it makes
Were obvious all along

283
The court may then rule
An injunction, or not
Against you, against them
For who knows why and what

284
The court may award damages
Or minimally royalties
Depending on how much you
Win the court's loyalties

285
The court may award court
     fees
In exceptional cases
Like ripping up patents
And throwing into faces

286
You can only collect damages
For up to six years
Get those lawyers going
And spread the good cheer

287
You can mark things protected
By writing on them "pat."
And the number; you won't
     collect
Damages without that

288
If part of the patent is
Found to be invalid
The rest still applies
Like a steak without salad

289
Design patents are also
Protected by all of this
You have to pay minimum
Two hundred fifty damages

290
When patents are challenged
Some letters are then sent
They're also sent out for
Any case of infringement

291
In a clash of two patents
The first one prevails
The other is corrected
And all that entails

292
Mismarking as patented, or
Claiming when not,
Is a fine of up to five
Hundred dollars, hot shot

293
If you're living abroad
Just send one of your staff
Who lives here to sue for you
On your behalf

294
Instead of the courts
You can use arbitration
If both of the parties
Give affirmation

295
An item that can be made
In a patented way
Is assumed to have been so
Which seems backwards, I say

296
States are like people
When suing in courts
They're liable for actions
Infringeable, all sorts

297
An invention promoter
Can help you with issues
You can sue if his promises
Were all made of tissues

301
If you recognize an invention
In whole or in part
You can file a complaint
And then claim "prior art"

302
You can also request
On the very same day
A reexamination, if
You're willing to pay

303
The Director will think
And he'll squint and he'll
    scratch
And he'll try to decide if
The arguments match

304
And he may even open some
More patent questions
He'll also listen to the
Patent owner's suggestions

305
The owner may then change
The patent specific
To exclude prior art, in
Which case, it's terrific

306
Or he may try to send
An appeal of some sort
All actions get noted down
On the report

307
In the end, a certificate
Is issued in writing
The judgment is final
No crying, no fighting

311
This section is like the last one
But "Inter parte"
Which means that the
    questioner
Doesn't go away

312
See, "Ex parte" means
That a question is asked
And then the Director
Completes the whole task

313
Otherwise they're the same
Which explains my objection
To simply repeating all
I wrote the last section

314
Instead the Director
Sits back in his chair
And watches the fighting
And ensures it's all fair

315
And appeals can be filed
Which is very revealing
Because the procedure
Is hardly appealing

316
When everything's over
A certificate's written
On which party bited
And which one got bitten

317
If you lose your brought case
You don't get to make more
Unless you have new news
Which changes the score

318
The patent owner may also
Stay more litigation
Unless it will benefit
Some part of the nation

Part IV

351
This part is all about
Patenting treaties
With neighboring countries,
Those cute little sweeties

361
The office of patents
Does business with all
Countries and citizens
International

362
The office can collect fees
For other nations
And also take from them
Without reservation

363
International patents
Are also stored here
On the date they're recorded
By month, day, and year

364
All services rendered
For all other nations
Are according to treaties
And recommendations

365
The dates on the patents
Are from the dates filed
In any valid country
But not those reviled

366
International claims
Can still be withdrawn
Unless made nationally
Before they are gone

367
And there still are reviews
As treaties specify
If a claim gets misplaced,
Or held up, or denied

368
If a patent that's foreign
Is secretly kept
You can't tell its contents
To people inept

371
We respect foreign patents
And register them, sir
We respect them more than we
Respect foreigners

372
Our procedures are guided by
Treaties real, not fictitious
This chapter is becoming
Quite repetitious

373
For instance, this says that
We only accept
Forms from those people we
Accept, not reject

374
And we publish these too, just
Like all of the others
Because we really just love you
So, so much (oh, brother!)

375
We'll enforce foreign patents
As if we had written them
And the original language
Trumps ours, in a problem

376
All services rendered
Cost dollars, which fits
I assume that the payer is
The one who submits

Well that's it, hope you've
learned
All you wanted to know
If you have any problems
Please don't tell me so

Patent and Trademark Depository Libraries

Alabama

Auburn University Libraries
231 Mell Street
Auburn University, AL
    36849-5606
334-844-1738

Birmingham Public Library
2100 Park Place
Birmingham, AL 35203-2974
205-226-3610

Alaska

Anchorage Municipal Libraries
Z. J. Loussac Public Library
3600 Denali Street
Anchorage, AK 99503-6093
907-562-7323

Arizona

Noble Science and Engineering
    Library
Arizona State University
P.O. Box 871006
Tempe, AZ 85287-1006
480-965-6164

Arkansas

Arkansas State Library
P.O. Box 2040
State University, AR 72467
870-972-3077

California

California State Library
Library-Courts Building
P.O. Box 942837
Sacramento, CA 94287
916-653-6033

Los Angeles Public Library
Downtown Los Angeles
630 W. Fifth Street
Los Angeles, CA 90071
213-228-7000

San Diego Public Library
1105 Front Street
San Diego, CA 92101-3904
619-531-3900

San Francisco Public Library
100 Larkin Street (at Grove)
San Francisco, CA 94102
415-557-4400

Sunnyvale Center for
    Innovation, Invention, and
    Ideas
465 S. Mathilda Avenue
Suite 300
Sunnyvale, CA 94086
408-730-7290

Colorado

Denver Public Library
10 W. Fourteenth Ave. Pkwy
Denver, CO 80204
303-691-0458

Connecticut

Hartford Public Library
500 Main Street
Hartford, CT 06103
860-543-8628

New Haven Free Public
    Library
133 Elm Street
New Haven, CT 06510
203-946-8130

Delaware

University of Delaware Library
181 South College Avenue
Newark, DE 19717-5267
302-831-2965

District of Columbia

Founders Library
Howard University
500 Howard Place, NW
Washington, DC 20059
202-806-7234

Florida

Broward County Main Library
100 S. Andrews Avenue
Fort Lauderdale, FL 33301
954-357-7444

Miami-Dade Public Library
101 W. Flagler Street
Miami, FL 33130
305-375-2665

Tampa Campus Library
University of South Florida
4202 E. Fowler Avenue
LIB 122
Tampa, FL 33620-5400
813-974-2726

University of Central Florida
    Libraries
P.O. Box 162666
Orlando, FL 32816
407-823-2562

Georgia

Georgia Institute of Technology
Price Gilbert Memorial Library
Atlanta, GA 30332-0900
404-894-4508

Hawaii

Hawaii State Library
478 S. King Street
Second Floor
Honolulu, HI 96813-2994
808-586-3477

Idaho

University of Idaho Library
Moscow, ID 83844-2350
208-885-6584

Illinois

Chicago Public Library
400 South State Street
Chicago, IL 60605
312-747-4450

Illinois State Library
Springfield, IL 62703
217-782-5859

Indiana

Indianapolis-Marion County
    Public Library
P.O. Box 211
Indianapolis, IN 46206
317-269-1700

Siegesmund Engineering
    Library
Purdue University
1530 Steward Center
West Lafayette, IN 47907
765-494-2800

Iowa

State Library of Iowa
1112 East Grand Avenue
Des Moines, IA 50319
515-281-4105

Kansas

Ablah Library
Wichita State University
1845 Fairmount
Wichita, KS 67260
316-978-3155

Kentucky

Louisville Free Public Library
301 York Street
Louisville, KY 40203
502-574-1611

Louisiana

Troy H. Middleton Library
Louisiana State University
53 Middleton Library
Baton Rouge, LA 70803
225-388-8875

Maine

Raymond H. Fogler Library
University of Maine
Orono, ME 04469-5729
207-581-1678

Maryland

Engineering and Physical
    Sciences Library
University of Maryland
College Park, MD 20742
301-405-9157

Massachusetts

Boston Public Library
P.O. Box 286
Boston, MA 02117
617-536-5400

Physical Sciences Library
University of Massachusetts
Amherst, MA 01003
413-545-1370

Michigan

Abigail S. Timme Library
Ferris State University
1010 Campus Drive
Big Rapids, MI 49307-2279
231-591-3500

Great Lakes Patent and
    Trademark Center
Detroit Public Library
5201 Woodward Avenue
Detroit, MI 48202
313-833-3379 or 800-547-0619

Media Union Library
University of Michigan
Ann Arbor, MI 48109-2136
313-764-5298

Minnesota

Minneapolis Public Library
300 Nicollet Mall
Minneapolis, MN 55401-1992
612-630-6120

Mississippi

Mississippi Library
    Commission
1221 Ellis Avenue
Jackson, MS 39209
877-594-5733 or 601-961-4120

Missouri

Linda Hall Library
St. Louis Public Library
5109 Cherry Street
Kansas City, MO 64110-2498
816-363-4600 or 800-662-1545

St. Louis Public Library
Central Library
1301 Olive Street
St. Louis, MO 63103
314-241-2288

Montana

Montana Tech Library
University of Montana
Butte, MT 59701
406-496-4281

Nebraska

Engineering Library
University of Nebraska–
    Lincoln
Nebraska Hall, Room W203
2nd Floor West
City Campus 0516
Lincoln, NE 68588-4100
402-472-3411

Nevada

Clark County Library
1401 E. Flamingo Road
Las Vegas, NV 89119
702-733-7810

The University Libraries
1664 N. Virginia Street
Reno, NV 89557
775-784-6500, Ext. 257

New Hampshire

New Hampshire State Library
20 Park Street
Concord, NH 03301
603-271-2143

New Jersey

Library of Science and
    Medicine
Rutgers, The State University
    of New Jersey
165 Bevier Road
Piscataway, NJ 08854-8009
732-445-3850

Newark Public Library
3rd Floor, Main Library
5 Washington Street
Newark, NJ 07101
973-733-7779

New Mexico

Centennial Science and
    Engineering Library
University of New Mexico
Albuquerque, NM 87131-1466
505-277-4412

New York

Buffalo and Erie County Public
    Library
Lafayette Square
Buffalo, NY 14203
716-858-7101

Central Library of Rochester
    and Monroe County
115 South Avenue
Rochester, NY 14604
716-428-7300

Melville Library
Room 1101
SUNY at Stony Brook
Stony Brook, NY 11794
631-632-7148

New York State Library
Cultural Education Center
Albany, NY 12230
518-474-5355

Science, Industry and Business
    Library
New York Public Library
188 Madison Avenue (at 34th
    Street)
New York, NY 10016
212-592-7000

North Carolina

D. H. Hill Library
North Carolina State
     University
2205 Hillsborough Street
Box 7111
Raleigh, NC 27695-7111
919-515-2935

North Dakota

Chester Fritz Library
University of North Dakota
University Avenue and
     Centennial Drive
P.O. Box 9000
Grand Forks, ND 58202
701-777-4888

Ohio

Akron-Summit County Public
     Library
1040 E. Tallmadge Avenue
Akron, OH 44310
330-643-9000

Cleveland Public Library
325 Superior Avenue, N.E.
Cleveland, OH 44114-1271
216-623-2800

Ohio State University Library
1858 Neil Avenue Mall
Columbus, OH 43210
614-292-6154

Public Library of Cincinnati
800 Vine Street
Cincinnati, OH 45202-2071
513-369-6971

Wright State University
     Library
Paul Laurence Dunbar Library
Dayton, OH 45435
937-775-2380

Oklahoma

Oklahoma State University
     Library
Stillwater, OK 74078-1071
405-744-0729 or 877-744-9161

Oregon

Paul L. Boley Law Library
Northwestern School of Law of
     Lewis and Clark College
10015 SW Terwilliger Blvd
Portland, OR 97219
503-768-6786

Pennsylvania

Carnegie Library of Pittsburgh
4400 Forbes Avenue
Pittsburgh, PA 15213
412-622-3138

Free Library of Philadelphia
1901 Vine Street
Philadelphia, PA 19103
215-686-5331

Penn State University
Paterno Library, Business
     Library
University Park, PA 16802
814-865-6369

Puerto Rico

General Library
Bayamon Campus
University of Puerto Rico
Bayamon, PR 00959
787-786-5225

University of Puerto Rico at
     Mayagüez
P.O. Box 9022
Mayagüez, PR 00681-9022
787-832-4040, Ext. 2022

Rhode Island

Providence Public Library
225 Washington Street
Providence, RI 02903
401-455-8027

South Carolina

R. M. Cooper Library
Clemson University Library
Box 343001
Clemson, SC 29634-3001
864-656-3024

South Dakota

South Dakota School of Mines
     and Technology
Devereaux Library
501 East St. Joseph Street
Rapid City, SD 57701-3995
605-394-1275

Tennessee

Memphis/Shelby County
Public Library and Information
     Center
1850 Peabody Avenue
Memphis, TN 38104
901-725-8877

Stevenson Science and
     Engineering Library
Vanderbilt University
419 21st Avenue South
Nashville, TN 37240
615-322-2717

Texas

Fondren Library
Rice University
P.O. Box 1892
Houston, TX 77251-1892
713-348-5483

Texas (Cont.)

Government Information
    Center
1515 Young Street, 6th Floor
Dallas, TX 75201
214-670-1468

San Antonio Public Library
600 Soledad
San Antonio, TX 78205
210-207-2500

Sterling C. Evans Library
Texas A&M University
College Station, TX 77843-5000
979-845-5745

Texas Tech University
    Libraries
18th and Boston
P.O. Box 40002
Lubbock, TX 79409-0002
806-742-2282

University of Texas at Austin
McKinney Engineering Library
ECJ 1.300
Austin, TX 78713
512-495-4500

Utah

University of Utah Marriott
    Library
295 S 1500 E, Level 1
Salt Lake City, UT 84112-0860
801-581-8558

Vermont

Bailey/Howe Library
University of Vermont
Burlington, VT 05405
802-656 2542

Virginia

James Branch Cabell Library
Virginia Commonwealth
    University
901 Park Avenue
P.O. Box 842033
Richmond, VA 23284-2033
804-828-1104

Washington

University of Washington
Engineering Library
P.O. Box 352170
Seattle, WA 98195-2170
206-543-0740

West Virginia

Evansdale Library
West Virginia University
P.O. Box 6105
Morgantown, WV 26506-6105
304-293-4695, Ext. 5113

Wisconsin

Kurt F. Wendt Library
University of Wisconsin–
    Madison
215 N. Randall Avenue
Madison, WI 53706-1688
608-262-6845

Milwaukee Public Library
814 W. Wisconsin Avenue
Milwaukee, WI 53233
414-286-3151

Wyoming

Wyoming State Library
2301 Capitol Avenue
Cheyenne, WY 82002-0060
307-777-6333

Index

Timothy Lee Wherry joined the faculty of Penn State University in 1990 following nine years as a librarian in private industry, a large public library, and academia. In these previous assignments, his responsibilities included providing engineering, scientific, business, and patent-related information to library users. Wherry continues to conduct research and to work with academics in the fields of engineering, business, and science. His interests are in patent research and the problems of intellectual property protection in the digital age, and he has published a number of articles and books on these topics. Wherry has held the positions of Assistant Dean for Information Services and Head of Learning Resources at Penn State's Altoona College, and he is currently Director of the Robert E. Eiche Library at Penn State Altoona.